Sunset

Tax$aver
Automobile

By Jay Knepp, CPA
Tax Specialist

Lane Publishing Co. ■ Menlo Park, California

Edited by Fran Feldman
Coordinating Editor: Linda Selden
Design: Brooklyn Graphic
Cover Design: Design Systems Group

Sunset Books
  Editor: David E. Clark
  Managing Editor: Elizabeth L. Hogan

First printing January 1987

From Coopers & Lybrand

We have reviewed *Automobile Tax$aver* for accuracy in its
description of federal income tax law.

Based on our interpretation of the Internal Revenue Code
(including 1986 amendments) and its regulations, public rulings,
and court decisions, we believe that *Tax$aver* accurately
describes and interprets the applicable provisions of the law.
Any taxpayer who follows the guidance of *Tax$aver* will have
appropriate documentation to support his or her auto-related
deductions.

However, it is important to recognize that federal income tax
laws and application of the Internal Revenue Service code and
regulations are often a matter of interpretation. As a result, an
Internal Revenue Service agent examining a taxpayer's return
may disagree with the treatment of certain items of income and
deductions as covered in this book. Because tax laws are continually subject to change by legislation, Internal Revenue
Service regulations, public rulings, and court decisions, we cannot guarantee that a position taken by a taxpayer based on
information in this book will not be successfully challenged by
the Internal Revenue Service. In addition, individual facts and
circumstances may result in an outcome different from that
anticipated.

In view of the complexities of the tax laws and varying inter-
pretations, taxpayers should not rely solely on the advice con-
tained in *Tax$aver*, but should use it in conjunction with advice
from their own tax advisor.

*(Coopers & Lybrand is an international accounting firm with 98
offices in the United States.)*

Table of Contents

Contents (Cont'd.)

Tax Help

Index

If you drive an automobile in any one of the many ways which can produce tax deductions, then *Automobile Tax$aver* is for you. It's a unique combination of tax advice and information together with a systematic record-keeping system that's designed to give the IRS the records and documentation it demands—and, in some cases, even more.

This book, specifically created with the automobile in mind, is designed for *you*, not for a tax specialist. It contains complete tax information on the situations, whether business related or not, you might encounter as an auto user and tells you what you can deduct, how to keep required records easily and simply, and how to prove your claims should you be audited. Changes resulting from the passage of the Tax Reform Act of 1986 are highlighted in the text.

Above all, the book helps you minimize your taxes by showing you how to claim every deduction you deserve—the goal of all taxpayers.

Deductible Automobile Expenses

Most of the people who claim auto deductions are using cars in business-related activities. But you may also be able to take a deduction for other uses and expenses that you incur.

Business-related expenses. Taxpayers who use their own car, a leased car, or a company car in connection with their trade or business, whether they're reimbursed or not, can claim auto deductions. This includes people who are employees or self-employed, companies (incorporated or not), executives, officers, and professionals. Investors, such as those in securities or real estate, and people who produce, collect, or preserve income can also deduct automobile expenses, though there are some special rules for investment activity.

Many taxpayers, especially those in outside sales, can claim both local business transportation expenses and away-from-home travel expenses. If you use an auto only for local business entertainment, you are entitled to very specific deductions. And if you have an office at home, what might otherwise be considered as nondeductible commuting expenses are deductible for you.

Perhaps you lease rather than own a car. The IRS considers many leases of luxury automobiles as a purchase and requires they be treated as such tax-wise, which can be to your disadvantage.

If you're an employee who is provided with a company car, you need to be concerned about whether its use is a taxable fringe benefit under current and proposed regulations. And as an employee, you can legally deduct any job-related expenses, including auto use, which are necessary to do your job properly. They must be of primary benefit to you, not your employer.

Expenses that may or may not be business related.
Taxpayers who incur moving, educational, or job-hunting expenses—assuming they meet all the other tests and rules—may deduct auto use connected with them. And if you had an auto stolen, suffered major damage from an act of God, or incurred some other casualty, you may have a deduction as well.

Nonbusiness-related expenses. Most taxpayers have some auto expenses connected with making charitable contributions to one or more of the many tax-exempt organizations. Whether you're an employee of the organization or a volunteer, a part-time or full-time worker, and are reimbursed or not, these auto expenses are deductible. The same may be true for travel for medical, dental, and many other health-related purposes.

Also keep in mind that you can deduct some nonbusiness auto expenses—interest on a loan and property taxes—on Schedule A, Form 1040 as itemized deductions. Beginning in 1987, interest on consumer loans is being phased out over a 4-year period.

The Importance of Good Records

Higher prices of both automobile ownership and operation have naturally led to greater deductions being claimed by taxpayers. Congress and the IRS have long been concerned about taxpayers, both corporate and individual, using business cars for personal purposes. As a result, they require you to determine what percentage of your car's use is for business. Also, current tax forms include some difficult auto-use questions for all taxpayers, no matter what their status. You must answer questions about all business, personal, and commuting miles driven, and about the evidence you have to support your claims. Most importantly, you'll also be asked if you have *written* records.

With this book, you'll be armed not only with knowledge but also with excellent documentation.

Permanent annual records. The tax information and forms included in this book are designed for one year's use. The reasons for this are simple and logical. Tax laws change constantly and starting a new book each year enables you to keep up to date with changes in tax law, as well as current developments. It reduces the chance you'll waste time and energy keeping records which are no longer required, or fail to meet some new requirement, which could prove costly. Also, with a permanent annual record, you'll always be prepared in the event the IRS questions your return.

Keeping abreast of tax law. Laws and regulations pertaining to assets used for both business and personal purposes change rapidly and often. In addition, court decisions are continually influencing and reinterpreting tax law. Relevant court decisions are presented in this book to help you understand why other taxpayers won or lost when they went to court. Be aware, however, that certain court decisions aren't binding in all jurisdictions.

But many areas in tax law are simply too complex for the average taxpayer. It's always wise to consult a competent professional tax advisor about any situation that concerns you, especially where large amounts of money are involved. For this reason, we've included a section to help you choose a tax advisor.

Tax terms. Baffled by the complicated terms used by the IRS in their tax forms and publications? In order to comply with all the regulations, it's essential to understand and speak their language. For definitions of the most commonly used terms, consult the glossary beginning on page 140. ■

Records & Methods

Whether you're preparing your own tax return, turning your records over to a professional tax advisor, or facing an audit by the IRS, complete tax records maintained in an orderly, organized fashion are essential. These records must substantiate your claims, especially the percentage of business use.

It's no secret that many taxpayers regard this work as tedious and unpleasant. But once you know what constitutes good records and how to keep them, and you understand how to use the specially designed forms in this book (all of which meet current IRS record-keeping requirements), you can make the tough IRS rules work *for* you, not against you.

What are adequate records? The IRS does not require you to keep records in any particular form or by any special method. They say only that you must have adequate records and sufficient evidence which, in combination, can prove each element—the amount, date, place, and business purpose—of an expenditure.

Receipts are ordinarily the best evidence to prove the *amount* of an expense. You can prove the *time* element by recording the date of each expense or use (if away from home, record the inclusive days of the trip). The *place* element can be proven by indicating where the use occurred. Document the *business purpose* by recording the business reason for the auto's use or the nature of the benefit gained or expected. (Unless the business purpose of an expense is clear from the surrounding circumstances, a written statement is generally required.)

Entertainment expenses require a fifth element of proof—*business relationship*. You need to show the name, title, company name, or some other designation sufficient to establish the business relationship to you.

These records should be permanent, accurate, complete, and supported by documents that clearly establish the nature and intent of the

9

expense. Remember, however, that any record or evidence is not the sole determinant of deductibility. The facts and circumstances of each case will often dictate the final tax result.

How elaborate your records are depends on your individual situation. However, entries on a desk calendar or canceled checks alone are not usually considered as proper proof when unsupported by other documentary evidence.

When to make entries. The IRS is emphatic that records written at or near the time the expense occurs and supported by sufficient documentary evidence are much more credible than evidence reconstructed later. According to temporary regulations now in effect, log entries do not have to be contemporaneous, but the rules do state that "a log maintained on a weekly basis, which accounts for use during the week, shall be considered a record made at or near the time of such use."

This regulation means you can accumulate your receipts and notes, and make all entries in a log *once* a week. Sampling techniques (see page 64) that allow you to maintain records for

only a portion of the year can make record keeping even easier for you.

How to keep good records. This book provides all the specific instructions and forms you'll need for keeping your records. Always have it with you. Since your records will have the highest degree of credibility if maintained close to the time the use or expense occurs, decide on when it's most suitable for you to make entries and develop a routine. Don't rely on memory—it's easy to forget cab fares, tips, phone calls, and other incidental expenses, all of which add up over a period of time.

Tax$aver Tip. *An excellent way to keep track of expenses, regardless of how paid, is to use a portable tape recorder. That way, you can tape-record your activities and expenses during the week, then enter all the information in this book the following Monday morning. It's a good idea to initial and date the entry.*

Here are some additional record-keeping hints which may be of help:

- Always pay by check or credit card if possible, since you're instantly creating a useful record.
- Always ask for a receipt, especially when paying cash, and keep all receipts on file.
- When you can't get a receipt for a cash payment, record and explain the payment in your records as soon as possible after the expenditure.
- Though most expenses should be recorded separately, some incidental travel costs can be totaled by categories; for these you can make *one* entry for the entire day. You don't have to record the business purpose of each expense.
- Tips can be recorded separately or included with the cost of the services received.
- Never deduct expenses the IRS may consider lavish or extravagant.

How long to retain records. All logs, checkbooks, canceled checks, receipts, and tax returns should be retained for at least 3 years from the date of filing, the usual length of time the IRS may select a return for audit. However, if it's found that some income was not reported and it's greater than 25%

of what was reported, the period available for audit is 6 years after the return was filed. And the IRS can go back to *any* year when no return is filed, a return is false or fraudulent, or criminal activity is suspected.

Retain the following records indefinitely:

1. Records that pertain to income-averaging when you need the information for the base period years (repealed, effective 1987)
2. Records that relate to the basis of property subject to depreciation which is needed to figure the gain or loss on sale of the asset, or the basis of new property when a trade-in is involved
3. Property records required to figure the amount of depreciation or investment tax credit recapture due to sale or disposition of the property before the end of its estimated useful life

You'll also need records from prior years in the following cases:

1. If you file a claim for a refund for taxes you've overpaid
2. If you need to amend a prior year's return
3. If changes in tax law entitle you to benefits only on the basis of previous years' records

11

Often, records can also be helpful to the executor of your estate.

If a prior year's return is lost or misplaced, you can get a copy from the IRS. Ask for Form 4506—Request for Copy of Tax Form.

Lastly, secure *all* records (tax returns, your *Tax$aver*, and all other evidence) relating to a specific tax year in an envelope or some other convenient form and store it in a safe place.

Penalties for understatement of tax liability. Whenever noncompliance with tax laws results in an underpayment of tax due to negligence or intentional disregard of rules and regulations, you're subject to a penalty equal to 5% of the amount of the deficiency related to negligence, interest, and an additional penalty equal to 50% of the interest due on the underpayment. Under the provisions of the Tax Reform Act of 1986, the penalty for substantial understatement of tax liability is 20% of the amount of the understatement, and the penalty for any amount attributable to fraud is 75% of the amount of the deficiency related to fraud. Both penalties apply to returns required to be filed on or after January 1, 1987. ■

Without a doubt, knowing and proving the percentage of time you used your car for business, called your business use percentage (BUP), is the single most important step you can take regarding deductible business driving. To achieve maximum tax benefits, your goal is to keep it as high as possible and *never* allow it to be *50% or less.*

In the past, many taxpayers simply estimated their BUP. The IRS regularly accepted these estimates, sometimes determining their own, to calculate the deductible business portion of all expenses associated with a car. Now, taxpayers are required to figure their BUP directly on IRS forms. The reasons for this requirement are twofold: first, the higher cost of owning a car has naturally resulted in larger deductions; and second, more and more taxpayers have been deducting *personal* use of an automobile as a business expense.

As a result, tax law pertaining to the use of a car for business travel and entertainment has undergone major revision. Congress has ordered the IRS to assess and collect penalties on taxpayers who "claim tax benefits far in excess of what can be justified."

To address this problem, recently adopted temporary regulations limit tax benefits and depreciation deductions for cars used solely or partially for business. On Form 2106, employees are required to answer the following questions:

- What is your daily and annual commuting mileage?
- Do you (or your spouse) have another vehicle available for personal purposes?
- If your employer provided you with a vehicle, is personal use during off duty hours permitted?
- Do you have evidence to support your deduction? If yes, is the evidence written?

If you're a taxpayer who uses Form 4562 to claim depreciation expenses, you'll also be asked if you have evidence, for all the listed property you're depreciating, to support the BUP claimed and if the evidence is written.

Determining your BUP. For the method most commonly used to compute BUP, you must know the following:

1. The total miles driven for *all* purposes during the year
2. The total miles driven for *qualified business use*—any use in trade or business, excluding miles driven for investment purposes as described on page 44

How do you derive these two mileage amounts? The best method is to write down your mileage on the first and last days of the tax year in the Record of Important Information & Dates (page 70), then keep careful track in the logs of all business miles driven during the year. The IRS has also approved some sampling techniques, as explained on page 64, for determining your BUP.

To arrive at your percentage, divide total business miles by the total of all miles driven, using the form on page 130. You'll need your BUP to compute your total auto deduction for the year when you keep track of your expenses using the actual cost method. If you're using the standard mileage rate instead, your BUP is still important for interest and property taxes (see page 22).

If you *add to* or *change* your activities but you're in business all year, you don't have to prorate the months. However, an employee who starts a business as a sideline during the year should count only those months the new business was actually in operation.

The 50% test. It's very important to keep your BUP (excluding investment use) above 50%. For each year that it's more than 50%, most negative effects of the test are eliminated. The one exception relates to the recapture of investment tax credit (see page 26). Let's say you claimed the credit for the year you bought the car prior to 1986 and your BUP that year was 80%. Now, suppose that the following year your business use falls to 60%, a proportional decrease of 25%. You must then recapture (pay back) 25% of the amount claimed the first year; further reductions in business use in later years are treated similarly.

Failure to meet 50% test the first year. What happens when you do *not* meet the 50% test the first year, i.e., your BUP (again with no investment use included) is 50% or less?

The IRS has established some listed property regulations, which apply to automobiles purchased or leased after June 18, 1984 (a passenger automobile that weighs 6,000 pounds or less and that is not used for hire to transport people or goods is considered listed property). Under the Tax Reform Act of 1986, if the 50% test is not met, the following listed property limitations apply for autos purchased and placed in service in a trade or business on or after January 1, 1987:

1. *No* Section 179 expense (see page 26) can be claimed.
2. *No* accelerated depreciation over a 5-year life is allowed.
3. Depreciation *must* be computed under the straight-line method.

The net result is that you're stuck with straight-line depreciation for as long as you keep the car. Your deductions can still increase if the BUP increases in subsequent years, but all other rates and methods are set. For more information on depreciation, see page 26.

Tax$aver Tip. *If you buy a car for business late in the year, with this short time period, you should be able to control the amount of business and personal mileage, easily document it, and arrive at a figure close to your desired BUP. If you're reasonably sure future business use will be very high, make the current BUP as high as possible.*

Failure to meet 50% test after first year. Suppose you met the 50% test the first year, claimed the tax credit (if allowable), and got the maximum depreciation deduction. If, in any succeeding year, your BUP falls to 50% or less, you're faced with the following:

1. Recapturing *all* investment tax credit previously claimed or whatever is left after other recapture rules have been applied
2. Recapturing *all* Section 179 expense previously claimed

15

3. Recapturing *all* depreciation previously claimed that is in excess of what would have been claimed under the straight-line method

4. Using the straight-line method for all remaining depreciation

Note that because your BUP fell to 50% or less in a succeeding year, you've lost all the benefits of tax credits and accelerated depreciation.

Tax$aver Tip. *To maximize your BUP, you may want to buy an economical second car and drive it for all or most personal purposes. Designate the more expensive car as the business car and drive it for personal use only when you have no choice.*

Special rules related to car ownership. If you're an employee using your own car, the use will not be considered qualified business use unless it's for the convenience of your employer. (Use for a substantial business reason of the employer during your regular working hours will usually satisfy this requirement.) Use of your car must also be required as a condition of employment, which means to perform your duties properly; yet your employer need not explicitly require the use. Though a written statement from your employer will help, IRS regulations state that "a mere statement by the employer that the use of the property is a condition of employment is not sufficient."

If the car is owned by the employer, all the listed property limitations discussed earlier apply (see also page 32). ■

The IRS allows taxpayers to use either of two methods to determine their total auto deduction for the year. The simplest one, the *standard mileage rate method* (SMR), is based on a fixed mileage rate established by the IRS. The second, the *actual cost method* (ACM), requires you to keep detailed records and itemize each expense. Regardless of the method you choose, the forms you'll need to keep track of your mileage and expenses, as well as to compute your deduction, are explained in the section beginning on page 63.

Under the Tax Reform Act of 1986, employees and outside salespeople claim these expenses on Schedule A, deducting only the amount that exceeds 2% of their adjusted gross income. They must also file Form 2106.

Standard Mileage Rate Method

SMR is the easiest record-keeping way to figure your deduction, since you simply keep track of actual business miles driven during the year and multiply the total by the rate allowed. Because the deduction per business mile is fixed by the IRS, your total deduction simply depends on how many miles you drive. This method is acceptable for cars, vans, pickups, and panel trucks.

You can only use SMR if all of the following apply:

1. You own the car.
2. You don't use more than one car at the same time in the same business.
3. You don't use the car for hire (such as a car available for rent or a taxi).
4. You've not claimed depreciation on the car in a previous year by any method other than straight-line.
5. You've never claimed a Section 179 deduction or other additional first-year depreciation in a prior year.
6. You bought the car, placed it in service after 1980, and elected SMR for the first year.

If you don't qualify for SMR, you'll have to use ACM (see page 20).

The rate currently authorized by the IRS is 21¢ for the first 15,000 business miles and 11¢ a mile thereafter. This amount is intended to cover most operating and fixed costs, including gas and oil, repairs and maintenance, garaging, supplies, licenses, insurance, and depreciation.

The IRS has not been very liberal in raising this rate—since 1977 it has increased an average of only 4.4% per year. Obviously, these increases have not kept up with the rising costs of buying, financing, or operating any kind of car. In fact, research has shown that the per mile cost of operating a car is much higher than the IRS rate.

Who can use SMR? In spite of the restrictions and limitations of this method, many employers use it for their reimbursement policy, since it requires a minimum of record keeping. (This does *not*, however, prevent employees from proving, by any method, that their expenses were greater than their reimbursements and deducting the excess.)

Employees, self-employed people, professionals, and outside salespeople also use SMR. An employee who is also a stockholder (even one who owns 100% of the corporation's stock) can use SMR.

How much can you deduct? You can apply the maximum rate of 21¢ per mile *only* against the first 15,000 business miles. Thereafter, the rate for all miles is 11¢. You can also deduct the business portion of interest and state and local taxes (but not gas tax). Parking fees and tolls are fully deductible.

If you own several cars and use one primarily for business and the others only occasionally for business, you must combine the business miles of all cars driven. If one is fully depreciated, you must use the 11¢ rate for that car. If you and your spouse own just one car but use it in separate businesses, you're still limited to 15,000 miles at the 21¢ rate. And if you replace a car during the year, you can combine mileages. If you wish, you can use ACM for the new car.

Tax$aver Tip. *If you and your spouse each use a car in different businesses, the cars should be separately owned so each person can deduct 15,000 miles at the 21¢ rate.*

Computing the deduction under SMR. Use this method for all business mileage—both local transportation and away-from-home travel. You only have to prove actual miles driven per your odometer readings.

Here's an example of how to compute the total automobile deduction using SMR. (This example assumes no reimbursements were received and the car was purchased in 1986.)

BUP Computation

Total miles driven in 1986	21,000
Total business miles driven	18,000
BUP (18,000÷21,000)=	86%

Mileage Computation

15,000 miles × 21¢ rate	$3,150
3,000 miles × 11¢ rate	330
Subtotal	$3,480

Other Expenses

Business parking fees in full	$ 420
Business tolls in full	180
Subtotal	$ 600
Interest on car loan	$ 720

Sales tax on purchase*	480
Personal property tax	125
Subtotal	$1,325
Subtotal × BUP ($1,325 × 86%)=	1,140
Total 1986 Deduction	**$5,220**

*Repealed, effective January 1, 1987

As far as depreciation and SMR are concerned, you need to be aware of only a few details, since the IRS already includes in SMR depreciation at the rate of 8¢ per mile. When you use SMR the first year, you're choosing to *never* use an accelerated method of depreciation for that car. When you use SMR and sell a car or trade it in, you must use the applicable depreciation rate per business mile for each year as a reduction of your original cost basis, just as if depreciation for each year had been claimed separately. The rate per mile was 7¢ for 1980–81, 7½¢ for 1982, and 8¢ thereafter.

Any car used by a taxpayer who uses SMR is considered to be fully depreciated after 60,000 business miles have been claimed. Thus, it takes at least 4 years to fully depreciate a car.

The IRS is simply saying that you can eventually deduct 60,000 miles at the 21¢ rate; every mile after that, for *that* car, must be deducted at the 11¢ rate.

Tax$aver Tip. *Once your car is fully depreciated under the rules and only the 11¢ per mile rate is available to you, you're probably better off itemizing your expenses under ACM, even without depreciation, since it's likely to result in a larger deduction.*

Actual Cost Method

ACM requires that you keep an adequate record of all the actual operating and fixed costs, such as gas and oil, repairs and maintenance, interest, insurance, and, most importantly, depreciation (see page 67 for a checklist of deductible auto expenses). Whether you choose ACM or have to use it, you must have evidence to prove those expenses.

If a car is used exclusively for business, you can deduct all the costs of operation. Typically, however, the car is used for both business and personal use, so an allocation of expenses must be made. Only the ordinary and necessary expenses directly attributable to business are deductible.

The IRS says that any car expenses of a personal nature, including commuting between your home and your regular place of business, are not deductible. The purchase price of a car *cannot* be deducted in full but must be depreciated over the car's estimated useful life. This also applies to any major addition or replacement which either adds value to the car or will last longer than a year, such as a new engine, a cellular telephone, or a stereo tape player.

Who can use ACM? Generally, all taxpayers who are sure that ACM will result in the largest deduction use this method. But you may not have a choice, since you *must* use ACM if *any* of the following apply to you:

1. You lease your car.
2. You use more than one car at the same time for the same business.

3. You use your car for hire.

4. You claimed depreciation on your car by any method other than straight-line.

5. You claimed any type of additional first-year depreciation.

Leasing a car and ACM. If you lease a car, you must use ACM to figure your deductions. Assuming you satisfy all the general IRS rules and keep good records, your lease payments plus any operating expenses the lease agreement says you must pay are deductible. New rules apply for cars placed in service after June 18, 1984 (see page 15).

To figure your deduction, multiply the percent of business use by total leasing expenses. Remember that you cannot deduct any portion of lease expenses which relates to commuting or any other personal use. Any advance payments or prepayments, even if called lease payments, cannot be deducted in the year paid; the IRS considers these types of payments to be applied against the purchase price, and they must be divided equally over the entire term of the lease.

In short, you're allowed to deduct one lease payment for each month the car was used for business in the tax year, plus any prorated advance or prepayments.

For more information, see the section on leasing beginning on page 28.

Computing the deduction under ACM. In most cases, this computation is a three-step procedure. A form for computing your deduction is on page 130.

1. Determine the percentage of business use of your car.

2. Determine the total amount of expenses for the year, not including business parking fees and tolls.

3. Multiply your total expenses by the business use percentage, then add parking fees and tolls to determine your deduction for the year.

If you used your car for business less than a full year, what expenses should you include in the total for the use period? Suppose you paid your $1,000 insurance premium or made any other payment for the full year in a month you didn't use your car for business. Simply prorate that expense to $500, for example, if you used your car for business only 6 months out of the year. Then apply the business use percentage.

Other Rules & Considerations

When you're computing your automobile deductions for the year, it's important to be aware of certain rules and deductions which relate to both methods.

Rules for switching methods. In general, the rules for switching methods are as follows:

1. After 1980, any car placed in service where ACM was used the first year, regardless of the depreciation method used, must continue to use ACM and cannot switch to SMR.
2. You must elect to use SMR the first year the car is in service in order to switch to ACM in subsequent years. If you do switch, depreciation *must* be computed under the straight-line method over the car's estimated useful life. You can then switch back and forth, using the method which results in the larger deduction, until the car is fully depreciated.

If you placed a car in service before 1981 and you're still using it for business, you can use either SMR or ACM on a yearly basis until the car is considered fully depreciated. From then on, you must use the 11¢ rate for all future business miles for that particular car.

Nonbusiness deductible expenses. Under both SMR and ACM, the nonbusiness portion of interest and property taxes is deductible only if you itemize your deductions. The Tax Reform Act of 1986 phases out the deduction for nonbusiness interest on consumer loans: 65% is deductible in 1987, 40% in 1988, 20% in 1989, and 10% in 1990. After 1990, there is no further deduction for nonbusiness interest on consumer loans.

Under the new law, sales tax on the purchase of a car, business or nonbusiness, is no longer deductible. If it's a business car, see page 27.

Car pools. Neither SMR nor ACM can be used unless you operate a car pool as a profit-seeking business. If so, you would report any payments received as income and most likely would use ACM to calculate your expenses. The common home-work-home car pool, whether or not you receive any payments from passengers and regardless of the amount of your expenses, is of no tax consequence and need not be reported on your return.

Investment tax credit. For taxpayers using either method, the investment tax credit was available for tax years through 1985, but only if the car was used more than 50% in a trade or business. For recapture rules, see page 26.

Reimbursements. Regardless of the method used, and whether or not your expenses are reimbursed, review the section on reimbursements beginning on page 46.

Record keeping. If you're using SMR, the essential items to record are date, business miles traveled, and business purpose of each auto use. With either SMR or ACM, you need to show the date you purchased your car or started using it for business purposes, and the original cost or other basis, such as its fair market value. You also need a record of the total miles driven during the year.

SMR vs. ACM: A Comparison

Many knowledgeable people applaud SMR for its simplicity and for the record-keeping time it saves. But is this praise appropriate? Does SMR save that much time?

Unless you drive a fully depreciated old klunker, you're probably better off using ACM.

The only extra work you need to do—beyond keeping the records you need for SMR—is to ask for receipts and *write down* your expenses.

If you qualify to claim deductions by more than one method, the only way to be sure of maximum deductions is to compute them both ways. Using the forms in this book, log your mileage and record all your expenses for a year. Figure your deductions using both SMR and ACM, then compare the results.

To illustrate this point, consider the following: You drove your car a total of 20,000 miles last year, 16,000 of which were for business purposes. Your business use percentage was 80% (16,000 ÷ 20,000). Here is a comparison of your deduction under both methods:

Standard Mileage Rate Method

15,000 miles × 21¢ per mile	$3,150
1,000 miles × 11¢ per mile	110
Business portion of interest and taxes ($1,376 × 80%)	1,101
Parking fees and tolls (in full)	125
Total Deduction	***$4,486***

Actual Cost Method

Depreciation (5 years, straight-line)	$3,000
Gas, oil, lubes	1,970
Repairs	400
Tires and supplies	200
Insurance	700
Registration and licensing	150
Auto club dues	100
Interest and taxes	1,376
Subtotal	$7,896
Subtotal × BUP ($7,896 × 80%)	$6,317
Parking fees and tolls (in full)	125
Total Deduction	**$6,442**

Comparison of SMR vs. ACM

Deduction under ACM	$6,442
Deduction under SMR	(4,486)
Additional deduction using ACM	**$1,956**

With ACM, the deduction is almost $2,000 more. Using an accelerated depreciation method instead of straight-line would result in even greater savings. Note that the operating cost is 40¢ per mile ($7,896 ÷ 20,000 miles).

Tax$aver Tip. *You should generally choose ACM if any of the following apply to you:*

1. *You bought or own an expensive new or used car.*
2. *You change cars every 3 years or less.*
3. *You have large repair bills in one tax year, and ACM is available to use.*

Remember this rule. When you choose ACM the first year the car is placed in service and you claim additional first-year depreciation or compute depreciation under any method other than straight-line, you may *never* use SMR until you buy another car. So if you want to retain the option of switching methods from year to year, using the one which produces the greatest tax savings, figure your depreciation using the straight-line method starting with the year your car is placed in service. ■

Deductible Expenses

Depreciation

This area of tax law, one of the most complicated, is replete with accounting and economic theory, countless effective dates, and constantly changing rules. Here we explain the terms relating to depreciation and some rules you need to know.

Depreciation is the process of deducting the cost or other basis of business or income-producing property over its estimated useful life. There's no deduction for personal use of business assets. Depreciable property must have a useful life of more than a year.

The *Section 179* election allows you to deduct up to $10,000 ($5,000 before 1987) of the purchase price of depreciable property the first year it's placed in service, as opposed to depreciating it over its useful life. The deduction is limited to the taxable income from the trade or business in which the asset is used. Any amount so deducted reduces the basis. The $10,000 limit applies regardless of the number of assets placed in service that year.

If your total investment exceeds $200,000, see your tax advisor.

The *investment tax credit* (ITC), designed to stimulate investment in certain business or income-producing assets, allowed a taxpayer a credit against taxes based on a percentage of the property's cost. ITC has been repealed, effective January 1, 1986, by the Tax Reform Act of 1986. However, certain recapture rules may apply if you took a credit on an asset placed in service before that date. The law also reduces the value of credits carried over from previous years by 17½% for 1987 and by 35% thereafter.

Rules and limitations. Prior to 1987, a car was 3-year property, and a taxpayer could choose either the 3-year accelerated method of depreciation with a fixed percentage or the straight-line method over 3, 5, or 12 years. However, Congress has limited the maximum depreciation and/or Section 179 deductions. For a car placed in service between June 18, 1984, and April 2,

1985, the deduction cannot exceed $4,800 the first year and $6,000 each year thereafter. For a car placed in service between April 3, 1985, and December 31, 1986, the first-year deduction cannot exceed $3,200 and $4,800 thereafter. And for one placed in service after December 31, 1986, only $2,560 is allowed the first year, $4,100 the second year, $2,450 the third year, and $1,475 thereafter.

Under the new tax law, a car is 5-year property. If you meet the 50% test (see page 14) and buy a car after December 31, 1986, you can depreciate it over 5 years, using the 200% declining balance method, with a switch to straight-line when it yields a larger deduction. Or you can elect to depreciate the car over 5 years using the straight-line method. If you don't meet the 50% test, you must use straight-line.

Regardless of the date the car was placed in service, the amount must be further reduced by applying your business use percentage. If it falls to 50% or less in a subsequent year or the property is converted to nonbusiness use, you'll have to recapture part of your prior depreciation deduction and use only the straight-line method in the future.

Deducting sales tax via depreciation. Though sales tax is no longer deductible under the new law, you can include it as part of the original cost of the car, which allows you to deduct the business portion of the tax through depreciation.

Other considerations. If any one of these situations applies to you, consult your tax advisor:

- ITC must be recaptured if a car is disposed of by sale, exchange, or conversion to personal use before the end of its useful life. Find out if recapture rules apply to you; postponing the sale or trade of a car could help you avoid them.
- Rules for depreciation and ITC are different for cars placed in service before 1984.
- Cars with an undepreciated basis at the end of 3 or 5 years (depending on when they were placed in service) can be depreciated in subsequent years, subject to the same dollar limitations and current business use percentage.

Keep track of basis and depreciation on the form on page 71. ■

Leasing an Automobile

If you're one of the many Americans who buys a new car every year or so, is always making payments, and never actually owns one free of debt, leasing may be for you. On the other hand, buying a car is wiser if you like to keep a car for 5 or 6 years. Also, it usually costs more to lease than to buy.

Why people lease cars. Someone once said, "You should own things that increase in value and lease those that decrease in value." Certainly, most cars do depreciate the moment you leave the dealer's showroom. When you lease a car, you also benefit from lower monthly payments and avoid the large down payment required for a purchase, since most leases require only 2 months' payment in advance.

Here are some other advantages to leasing:

1. The down payment money you save can be used or invested elsewhere.
2. You'll always be driving a late-model luxury car.
3. Leasing is usually desirable in periods of high interest rates.
4. You can easily budget your insurance and maintenance expenses.
5. You can save valuable time in buying, servicing, and reselling when you need a new car.
6. Your leasing agent can help you choose the right model and accessories for your driving needs, achieve the highest resale value, receive discounts on replacement parts and supplies, and perhaps reduce insurance costs. An agent can also buy a car for a lot less than you can, usually at fleet prices.
7. You may benefit from some tax advantages, though they're not that different from buying (see below).

The disadvantage of a true lease (not a disguised purchase) is that you have no equity when it's over, unlike the car owner who has a used vehicle to sell. You must also have the highest type of credit rating to lease a car.

When a lease is really a purchase. Just because an agreement is called a lease doesn't automatically convince the IRS that it's not a conditional sales contract. If it's found to be a conditional sales contract, all lease payments are applied to the purchase price, and depreciation will be calculated just as if you owned the car.

The IRS has issued seven conditions which indicate that a lease should be treated as a conditional sale for tax purposes. If *any one* of these apply to your agreement, you just bought—rather than leased—a car:

1. The agreement applies part of each "rent" payment toward an equity interest that you will receive.
2. You get title to the car after making all the required payments.
3. You must pay an amount close to the cost of the car over a time period that's much shorter than the expected useful life, and you may continue to use it for nominal payments for an additional amount of time approximating its remaining estimated useful life.
4. You pay rent that is much more than the car's current fair rental value.
5. You have an option to buy the car at a price that is low compared to its value at the time you may take advantage of the option. Determine value at the time of the agreement.
6. You have an option to buy the car at a price that is low compared to the total amount you are required to pay under the lease.
7. The lease designates some part of the "rent" payments as interest, or part of the "rent" payments are easy to recognize as interest.

If your intent is to enter into a true lease, make sure *none* of the above appears in your agreement. However, there is one exception: if, under a lease agreement, you placed a car in service between January 1, 1981 and December 31, 1983, your transaction is guaranteed by the IRS to be treated as a lease for tax purposes if certain requirements are met.

Terminal rental adjustment clause (TRAC). This is a clause in an agreement that requires or allows the lessor to adjust the final payment on the lease based on the difference between a projection of the car's value when the lease is signed and its actual value at the time of the final payment. The rules differ depending on whether the lease agreement is dated before or after October 16, 1984. Consult your tax advisor if this highly technical situation applies to you.

Types of leases. True leases, where you simply rent a car for a specific period of time, are called operating leases and are not conditional sales contracts. They're typically either open- or closed-end leases.

An open-end lease can either make you money or cost you money when the lease expires. When you sign the lease, a specified resale value is agreed to. If the car sells for more, you get the excess; if it sells for less, you owe the difference. This type of lease is usually the lowest in cost.

A closed-end lease allows you to turn in the car with *no liability* for its resale price. But there are some closed-end leases that protect you against any resale loss, yet allow you to share in resale gains.

Both types of leases usually establish maximum allowable mileage, penalties for turning in the car early or late, and full or partial maintenance and insurance programs. You can make a "down payment" if you wish, thereby lowering your monthly payment. And you can always buy the car when the lease expires.

Finally, be sure to ask your leasing agent about disposing of your present car, special rates

for low mileage, use of a loaner when your leased car has major unscheduled repairs, and the consequences of your car being stolen or damaged in an accident. You should have to pay only the amount of your deductible on your insurance policy.

Tax effects of leasing. It's simply not true that leasing a car gives you tax breaks not available to owners. The expenses of business driving are always deductible, whether you own or lease your car. All lease payments are deductible as long as they're directly attributable to business operations. As with any car, only the percentage of business use is deductible, not commuting or personal use.

Trying to create quicker write-offs through lease payments will usually be ineffective, due to the availability of accelerated depreciation. And because the IRS requires any advance lease payments to be deducted over the term of the lease, paying in advance doesn't work either. Of course, there are cases where legally deductible lease payments are higher than monthly depreciation expense.

Seemingly advantageous rental agreements between related parties (you and your corporation or you and a relative, for example) run into trouble if they're unreasonable in amount. Even if reasonable, it still must be proved that providing the car is necessary to the taxpayer's business.

The IRS has devised a concept called income inclusion that applies to luxury cars leased after June 18, 1984. Under this concept, the listed property rules discussed on page 15 may limit the amount of your deductible lease payments. In the long run, you're likely to find that lease costs yield substantially the same tax benefits as depreciation on a car you own.

Other considerations and recommendations. A new wrinkle in auto financing is a balloon loan, which is very much like a lease. With such a loan, you can reduce your monthly payments by at least 20%, thanks to a balloon payment due at the end which approximates the car's estimated resale value. You finance the entire purchase price and, at the end of the loan, you can either pay it off in cash or by refinancing, or perhaps sell the car for a profit. Of course, you can simply give it back to the lender, possibly paying a fee for excess mileage and for returning the car early.

Keep in mind these other leasing considerations:

- It's possible to sell your present car to a leasing company for cash and lease it back from them.
- You can lease a used car; if it's an antique, it could actually increase in value.
- If you turn in a car before the end of the lease, not only could there be early termination penalties, but also you may have to recapture investment tax credit and depreciation (see page 26).
- Shop around for the best terms before finalizing any lease.

If you're undecided about whether to buy or lease, have your tax advisor compute the tax savings by year for both a leased car and one you own; then make your choice based on the findings. If you decide to lease, make sure the lease is custom-tailored to your own needs. ■

Employee Use of a Company Car

If you're an employee or officer of a corporation, whether or not you're a stockholder (majority or minority), and you drive a company car, then it's especially important that you maintain complete records of auto use. Failure to do so can result in disastrous effects for both you and the corporation.

If the IRS audits the corporation and finds unsubstantiated expenses for which you have been reimbursed, the corporate deductions may be disallowed and additional tax may be due. And since you were reimbursed for a nondeductible expense, the payments are then classified as income to you, either as a dividend or additional compensation, and you'll owe additional personal income tax. Thus, both you and the corporation may end up paying additional tax, plus interest, on the *same* disallowed expenses.

Many companies have included a clause in their bylaws stating that any stockholder must reimburse the corporation for any expenses disallowed by the IRS. This not only provides cash to the corporation but also allows the stockholder to deduct the reimbursement as an expense of an income-producing activity.

Accounting for personal use. When you keep an accurate record of your mileage, business and personal, and a fair market value of the personal use is determined under the IRS rules, the corporation can treat the personal use amount as additional compensation to you reported on Form W-2; as a dividend to you, in which case the corporation does not deduct the value of the personal use; or as part compensation, part dividend.

Documenting your expenses. Adequate records and substantiation will eliminate disallowances due solely to poor record keeping. As for the problem of personal use, it depends on how the IRS evaluates the facts and circumstances of each case.

To protect both you and the corporation, you can include in the corporate minutes a statement similar to this one: "Sue Curtis has been provided with a (*description of auto and fair market value*) which is necessary for her duties as (*title or job description*), is for the convenience of the corporation, and is a condition of employment. It is recognized that there will be some personal use of this vehicle and that Ms. Curtis will supply the company with a mileage record of personal use. This mileage will be valued according to IRS rules, and the value so determined will be additional compensation and reported annually on her W-2 form. Ms. Curtis has also agreed to the withholding of all required taxes on this additional compensation." Make sure it's dated and signed by the corporation and the employee/stockholder. Of course, the title to the car must be in the corporation's name.

An alternative method is for the corporation to charge the employee/stockholder for the value of the personal use. You write a check (nondeductible) payable to the corporation, which then credits it against the operating expenses of the car. The net result is that the corporation is only deducting the business-related portion of the car's cost, which is exactly what the IRS wants.

Tax$aver Tip. *Perhaps the most logical plan for all concerned is to buy the company-owned car you're now using at the existing fair market value or at the undepreciated amount on the company's books, whichever you and the company agree on. Then ask the company to set up a reimbursement plan, using either the standard mileage rate or the actual cost method, again whichever is most advantageous for the corporation and yourself.*

Whether a car is driven by an employee or by an owner of the company, the listed property rules discussed on page 15 apply. However, there are special rules if you own more than 5% of the company. In that case, consult your tax advisor. ∎

Use of an Automobile as a Fringe Benefit

For many years, fringe benefits in general have been the single most volatile area of tax law. Temporary and proposed regulations were issued by the IRS in January, 1985, and were partly amended in February. When contemporaneous record-keeping requirements were repealed in April, the IRS withdrew the regulations and issued new proposed and temporary ones. These, too, have been extensively amended and are under review.

Since the rules change continually, we will offer only a cursory look at the subject as it pertains to automobiles. Generally, the current temporary regulations are effective retroactively to January 1, 1985.

Taxable fringe benefits. When your employer provides you with a car, the fair market value of its personal use is included in your gross income, unless specifically excluded from income by other tax law or unless you've paid the company for the value of your personal use. The regulations provide both general and special rules that can be used to determine fair market value.

The employee can use either the general or the special rules to value the benefit. If a special rule is used, it must be the same as that used by the employer. (This situation occurs when you use an employer-provided vehicle for both business and personal use and your employer included the full value of the car on your W-2 form.) You can then offset the income by claiming all your expenses on Form 2106. Under the provisions of the Tax Reform Act of 1986, any excess is taken as an itemized deduction on Schedule A and is subject to a 2% of adjusted gross income limitation.

Unless personal use of an employer-provided car is very minimal, you must report this use as a taxable fringe benefit (assuming the full value is not included on your W-2. Since the rules are complex, see your tax advisor if this situation applies to you.

Provision of fuel-in-kind may be valued at 5.5¢ per mile according to the regulations. Vehicles provided by employers for commuting have special optional valuation rules. This value is fixed at $1.50 for each one-way commute and applies to each person commuting in the vehicle. The employer must require that one or more employees commute in the car and have a written policy that it not be used for any but minimal personal purposes other than commuting. This rule no longer applies to control employees (directors, officers, or anyone owning 1% or more of the company)

Nontaxable fringe benefits. Automobile benefits you receive are excluded from income if they qualify as a *working condition fringe* or as a *de minimis fringe*. A working condition fringe is what would be deductible by you as an ordinary and necessary business expense had you paid for it yourself, such as the use of a company car or the value of free or reduced-cost parking on or near your employer's premises. If you sell cars and are provided with a demonstrator, you can exclude the value from income if the car is provided primarily to facilitate your job duties and if personal use of the car is substantially restricted.

A de minimus fringe is a benefit that is so minimal that accounting for it would not only be unreasonable but also administratively impractical. Occasional, infrequent personal use of a company car is considered a de minimus fringe.

Substantiation requirements. Whether you're including use of a car in income and deducting the expenses, or merely excluding fringe benefits from income, you must substantiate business and personal use of the car with sufficient evidence, just as you would to prove trade or business deductions.

Recommendation. If the issue of fringe benefits could affect you in a major way, consult your tax advisor. For more detailed information, obtain Publication 525: *Taxable and Nontaxable Income* from your local IRS office. ■

Local Transportation & Commuting Expenses

If you use a car or some other mode of transportation for business use, you'll need to know which transportation costs you can deduct and which costs, principally commuting, you cannot. Here's an explanation of what constitutes a local transportation expense and what constitutes a commuting expense.

Local Transportation Expenses

Local transportation expenses are those incurred in order to get from point A to point B anywhere in the immediate geographical area of your work or business, generally referred to as your tax home. This includes any trips during the work day *after* you arrive at work and *before* you depart for home, whether you're seeing customers or performing other business tasks, such as the pickup and delivery of inventory or supplies. (If you regularly work in two or more areas, you live away from your tax home, or you don't have a regular place of work, see your tax advisor.)

These local costs can be deducted, as long as they're ordinary and necessary, and related to the active conduct of any trade or business. Though these expenses typically relate to the operation and maintenance of your car (owned or leased), they can also include other forms of transportation, such as rail, bus, taxi, boat, or even airplane (commercial or private).

Local transportation does *not* include commuting—driving to your work site and returning home (see facing page).

Who deducts local transportation expenses?

Employers, employees, and people who are self-employed may deduct these expenses, depending primarily on who benefits from the payment. Typical occupations are outside salespeople, executives, and professionals. Beginning in 1987, employees and investors report these expenses together with other miscellaneous deductions on Schedule A and deduct only the excess of 2% of their adjusted gross income. Self-employed people use Schedule C.

Special rules for employees. According to the IRS, the general rule is that employees can treat local transportation as a business expense as long as it relates to their job. However, if the employee wishes to claim *any* depreciation (accelerated or Section 179), other requirements must be satisfied (see page 16).

Commuting Expenses

Since 1976, the IRS has attempted to implement very strict rules and definitions about commuting, local, and same-day business transportation. However, negative public reaction has resulted in an indefinite suspension of the effective date of those rulings.

Without any official word from the IRS, information and direction are being provided mainly by the courts. They say simply, "Commuting is commuting, regardless of the nature of the work engaged in, the distance traveled or the mode of transportation used."

The basic principle for any taxpayer is that travel (in the general area of your tax home) from your residence to your *first* job location and from your *last* job location to home is not a deductible expense, even when your first and/or last stop is your principal place of business, or a client or customer's place of business.

Exceptions to basic commuting rules. If your work assignment is minor or temporary, the daily transportation costs of travel between the area you normally work in and a location outside of this area are deductible. Temporary means the assignment must end within a fixed and reasonably short period of time; if it's definite from the beginning, it's considered a nondeductible commuting expense. If, after being temporary, the time period becomes definite, deductibility ceases at that time.

Permanent or indefinite assignments are not deductible, even when the job site is remote and no housing or public transportation is available nearby.

When a business trip by car requires that you be away from home one night, your travel costs are totally deductible and are *not* considered commuting. How far away from home must you travel? The Supreme Court has said simply that it's when you can't reasonably expect to leave from and return home at the start and finish of a day's work.

And you needn't be gone for an entire 24-hour period or only during dusk-to-dawn hours. The time period you're away should be such that you'd need to get sleep or rest.

Eliminating or reducing commuting. An excellent way to eliminate commuting restrictions is to use your home as your regular place of work. As long as you satisfy all the rules for deducting an office at home, you can deduct all your local transportation costs. You've eliminated those trips from residence to first job site and from last job location to home because you're already at *both* locations when the day begins. Your first and last stops are now deductible. Information on home office rules is available in *Sunset's Home Office Tax$aver.*

If you're not able to meet the home office rules, it's wise tax planning to live as close as possible to your regular place of business so you can minimize your nondeductible commuting expense.

Examples of nondeductible commuting. The courts have declared the following situations to be nondeductible:

- Carrying special equipment or tools to and from work, regardless of size or weight, storage facilities, or availability of public transportation

- Business discussions with business associates while driving to work

- Doing *any* kind of work in your car while driving to work, such as business calls from a cellular phone

- Car pools (see page 22)

- Cost of commuting in a company car, whether reimbursed or not

- Driving a car that displays advertising

- Driving to any regular place of employment, regardless of the distance traveled or the remoteness of the area

- Driving to a union hall, getting a work assignment, and driving to the job site for that day

- Teachers who make more than one trip from home to school each day

- Any taxpayers "on call" at home 24 hours a day, no matter where they drive or how many locations they visit

- Picking up or delivering anything at the first or last stop of the day (since no actual business is conducted, the IRS considers this nondeductible)

- Travel between a temporary residence and a regular place of employment

Tax$aver Tips. *Here are a few ideas that can save you tax dollars if they apply to your particular situation:*

- *Unless inconvenient, do any business driving required by your job **after** the first stop or **before** the last stop of the day.*

- *Have a written contract for any pickup or delivery arrangements.*

- *If having an office at home truly helps you do your job more efficiently or profitably, saves time, or provides any other benefit, ask your employer to give you a written statement that your office is for the convenience of the employer and is a condition of employment.*

- *When it's not reasonable or convenient to stop at the office before or after a long one-day trip outside your work area, you can deduct the costs of traveling from your home to the business location and back.*

- *Each day, try to make your first business stop on your way to your office and as close to home as possible. On your way home from the office, make your last stop a business one if you can, also as close to home as possible. This will reduce your personal miles.*

- *If you have two cars, you may want to consider designating the more expensive one as your business car and the other as your personal car. On days when you are reasonably sure to be driving a lot of business miles, use the business car. When you think you'll probably stay in the office or drive very little during the day, drive the personal car to work. This will also help you maximize the business use percentage of the business car.*

- *Another possibility is to keep your expensive business car **at work** and drive the personal car only to get there and back.* ∎

Combined Business & Pleasure Travel

In an audit, the IRS will look closely at any business trip where the trip might have combined business and pleasure. The rules below apply only to travel within the U.S.

Trips entirely for *business* reasons are fully deductible as long as the expenses incurred are ordinary and necessary. Conversely, trips entirely for *pleasure and personal* purposes offer no deductions at all. The gray area is when business and pleasure are combined. In this case, the IRS will try to determine what the "primary" purpose of the trip was; whether or not they allow the deductions depends on the facts and circumstances of each case.

What does "primary" mean? The most important consideration, according to the courts, is the *actual time* spent for business reasons compared with that spent on personal or pleasure activities. (Keep track of the hours spent on both in a diary.) Another consideration is the business destination's desirability as a resort area—the more preferred

your destination is as a vacation site, the more important your documentation becomes.

Primary purpose is business. Let's say you travel to San Francisco on business, but you also extend your stay for a short vacation. Though you can't deduct any vacation expenses, you or your company can still deduct the travel expenses to and from San Francisco, as well as other business expenses. In other words, deduct only the business expenses, just as if the trip were for business only. If you document the pleasure part of the trip, too, you'll have even better evidence if there's an audit.

Primary purpose is pleasure. Travel expenses for a trip whose primary purpose is pleasure are *not* deductible. However, once you get to your destination, you can always deduct expenses which are directly and properly for business reasons, just as if you were doing business at home. Even a strong secondary purpose, such as searching for income-producing property, will not turn a vacation into a business trip.

Convention expenses. You can deduct travel expenses to attend a convention if you prove that the benefits were to you and your trade or business and not to someone else. The convention should be clearly related to your business duties.

Under the Tax Reform Act of 1986, deductions for attending a convention or seminar for *investment* purposes are no longer allowable.

Tax$aver Tip. *Whether you're an employee or self-employed, plan to combine business with your next vacation. Document the results of your business meetings to show that the primary purpose was, in fact, business. To support your claims, get a signed statement from the businesspeople you contact on the trip, or write to them when you return home and keep copies of your letters. You or your company can then deduct the business portion of the trip.*

Travel expenses of spouse and family. When a spouse or other family member accompanies you on a business trip or to a business convention, it must be adequately shown that the person's presence on the trip has a distinct business, rather than social, purpose in order to deduct their travel expenses. Performing incidental services or helping entertain business associates are not acceptable business purposes.

When reimbursements for your spouse's expenses are received from your employer, the rules are the same as for you. The amounts are included in your income unless it's clearly established to be an ordinary and necessary corporate expense, and that the person's presence was of substantial benefit, not merely helpful, to the conduct of business. Unless these conditions are proven, the costs of a family member's travel, meals, and lodging are *not* deductible.

To help establish business purpose, consider obtaining a corporate resolution or statement detailing exactly what the person is to accomplish. Then keep a diary of everything the person does and how much time is spent doing it.

Your diary should describe in detail the activity that the person was engaged in: what services, if any, were contributed by the person and what meetings or social events the person attended. It's important to record the hours spent on each activity and to show whether the person's attendance was required or voluntary. You must also note the business reason or benefit that was expected or received.

One factor the courts will consider is whether or not the person assists in *nontraveling* business activities during the year. If so, it's wise to maintain a diary of the activities.

Tax$aver Tip. *Even if your spouse travels with you and you're not deducting spousal expenses, don't limit your lodging deduction to only half the double room rate. The IRS has said you can deduct the full cost of a single room, which usually results in a larger deduction. (Be sure to get proof of the single room rate.) The same rule applies to special two-party airfares.* ■

Use of an Automobile for Entertainment Purposes

Current tax law defines an "entertainment facility" as any property, real or personal, that is owned, rented, or used by a taxpayer for entertainment. This certainly can include a car or some other vehicle.

Before 1979, taxpayers who used their cars for business entertainment purposes could include the miles they drove for that reason in their total business miles for the year, thereby increasing the overall percentage of business use of their cars and resulting in larger annual deductions of all automobile expenses.

But in 1979, the Internal Revenue code was amended to state that "no deduction is allowed for any expense paid or incurred with respect to a facility which is used in conjunction with an activity which is of a type generally considered to constitute entertainment, amusement, or recreation." What this means is that you can no longer include mileage for entertainment purposes to increase the overall business use percentage of a car. But you can still deduct certain auto-related entertainment expenses. (Keep track of those expenses in the log on page 123.)

What is deductible? When you use a car for business entertainment, you are allowed to deduct all the direct expenses incurred as a result of that use, such as gas and oil, food, beverages, tolls, parking, and any other out-of-pocket expenses. They must only meet the general entertainment rules, such as the directly related or associated with tests.

Under the Tax Reform Act of 1986, only 80% of actual business meal and entertainment expenses is deductible, effective January 1, 1987. Business must be discussed during or directly before or after the meal. ■

Use of an Automobile for Investment Purposes

The Internal Revenue Code has a special section for taxpayers who deduct certain ordinary and necessary expenses if paid or incurred for the following reasons:

1. To either produce or collect taxable income
2. To manage, conserve, or maintain property held for the purpose of producing income
3. To determine, contest, pay, or claim a refund of any tax

Your expenses must be directly connected to one of these activities and the income must be taxable to you. Expenses related to the nontaxable income are not deductible. Deductible expenses should be reasonable relative to your overall investment activities.

What is ordinary and necessary? In income-producing activity, an expense is *ordinary* if it is customary, traditional, or usual, and *necessary* if found to be useful, helpful, or proper to the conduct of the investment business. Expenses also should be closely associated with the primary intention of producing income. A good way to prove your intent is to show what resulted from incurring the expense.

Effect of investment mileage on business use percentage. The tax law says that to claim accelerated depreciation on a car in the year it is placed in service, the car must be used more than 50% in a qualified trade or business. But it does *not* allow you to include investment mileage to reach that figure. Yet, if you meet the test *without* investment mileage, you can then add back your investment mileage, thereby increasing your business/investment use percentage and your overall deduction. Here's an example:

Your auto expenses total $6,800 (including depreciation) for the year. Your qualified business use mileage is 65%, investment mileage is 15%, and the rest is personal. Therefore, you meet the more-than-50% test and your allowable deduction is $5,440 ($6,800 × 80% [65% + 15%]).

Note that if the car is used 50% or less for business, only straight-line depreciation over a 5-year life is allowable. In this case, you can use both investment and business mileage in computing your business use percentage.

Record your investment miles in either the Log of Recurring Trips on page 73 or the Log of Nonrecurring Trips on page 78.

Where to report these deductions. Ordinary and necessary rental and royalty expenses of this nature are reported on Schedule E, Form 1040. Other investment expenses, whether they relate to securities transactions or any other type of investment, are deductible as miscellaneous deductions on Schedule A. Under the Tax Reform Act of 1986, these deductions are subject to a floor of 2% of adjusted gross income.

Deductible investment travel. The courts have found the following to be deductible:

- A taxpayer who deducted two of three trips, including meals and lodging, for the purpose of maintaining investment property
- An inventor who furthered the use of a patented invention by giving technical advice

- A taxpayer whose travel expenses were related to an unsuccessful attempt to purchase a racetrack but who was unable to obtain financing before the option to buy expired
- A taxpayer who investigated oil and mining leases and royalties, even though no property was acquired

Investment travel that was disallowed. In the following cases, the courts did not allow the investor to deduct travel expenses:

- A stockholder who traveled to the annual meeting of the company
- A taxpayer who made daily lunchtime trips to a brokerage office to watch the ticker tape
- An investor who made a week-long trip to a resort area where the investor attended 4 hours of investment seminars
- Taxpayers who traveled to properties they were trying to sell but who failed to prove the properties were held for the production of income ■

Reimbursed & Unreimbursed Expenses

Reimbursements for expenses, with few exceptions, must be either deducted from total allowable expenses or included in income, whether the reimbursements are received from employers, clients, passengers, or anyone else. Reimbursed or unreimbursed, and regardless of who eventually deducts them (employer or employee), deductible expenses must be ordinary and necessary to the operation of business. A form for recording reimbursements is on page 128.

Unreimbursed expenses or expenses that exceed reimbursements are reported with other miscellaneous deductions on Schedule A and are subject to a floor of 2% of adjusted gross income, effective in 1987.

Reporting on tax return not required. Suppose you properly account to your employer (by submitting a statement prepared from your daily records, along with receipts) and you're *fully reimbursed* for exactly the amount you spent. If the expenses were solely for the benefit of your employer, who then claims the deductions, you need *not* report any expenses or reimbursements. You do, however, have to keep records just as if *you* were claiming the expenses—you're simply reporting to your employer, not the IRS.

A few additional requirements for this nonreporting include the following:

1. You claim no added unreimbursed expenses on your return that relate to the same employer.
2. No personal expenses were reimbursed. (If they were, they must be considered as income.)
3. You and the employer are not related in any way.
4. You don't own more than 10% of the corporation's stock.

If you use the standard mileage rate and your reimbursements are equal to the 21¢ per mile rate, you are deemed to have made an accounting to your employer. You still must document the time, place, and business purpose of your expenses. There's no limitation on the number of miles driven under this arrangement.

Accounting to employer not required. Some employers simply pay a fixed amount each month for auto expenses. These amounts are basically treated as additional wages and should be included as income on your W-2 form, since withholding of taxes is required. Whether you use the actual cost method or the standard mileage rate, you can claim your auto expenses on Form 2106 as an offset to this income as long as you meet all required record-keeping rules. Without records, you'll end up paying tax on the reimbursements with *no* deductions.

Accounting to employer required. Many employers, as a matter of policy, require the reporting of actual expenses for reimbursement. Many also base auto expense reimbursements on the 21¢ per mile rate and use established per diem rates to cover other expenses, such as meals, lodging, laundry, cleaning, and tips. Because per diem rates do not cover cab fares, telegrams, or telephone calls, you can deduct these.

Note that if you're away from home on a temporary assignment, you can't use per diem rates to estimate allowable living expenses. You

also can't use per diem rates if you own more than 10% of the company's stock. Instead, you must account for all your expenses in full.

Your actual expenses for a trip are treated as "accounted for" if the per diem you receive doesn't exceed the maximum established rate for the area. You don't have to get receipts for travel expenses, but you or your employer must still have records of the mileage, time, place, and business purpose of the travel.

Be sure to keep duplicates of all receipts and expense reports since your employer could have the expenses disallowed because of inadequate or lost substantiation. Without your copies, the reimbursements could be treated as income, and you'd be forced to pay the tax even though you had legitimate offsetting expenses.

When reimbursements exceed expenses. If you're reimbursed for more than you spent, you account to your employer, your total reimbursements aren't included in your W-2 form, and you use the actual cost method, you need to include the excess in income on Form 1040; you need not file Form 2106. If your employer chooses to reimburse you more than 21¢ per mile, the *full* amount, not just the excess, must be reported on your W-2 form. You must then file Form 2106.

Use the method which gives you the largest amount to figure your expenses, so that any taxable excess is reduced as much as possible. If you use the standard mileage rate, the entire excess will be taxable unless the IRS can be convinced that the excess payment was necessary, reasonable, and due to unusual circumstances.

When expenses exceed reimbursements. This situation is more likely when you use actual costs and your employer reimburses you at the 21¢ per mile rate. You're required by the IRS to file a detailed statement with your return, even if you used the standard mileage rate; the statement must include all advances, allowances and reimbursements received, expenses paid by you, and charges paid or borne by your employer. Also include in the statement evidence that will establish the elements of your expenses. This statement will help prevent an audit, but if it doesn't, you're likely to be asked to substantiate *all* your travel and entertainment expenses.

Reimbursement available but not requested. Let's say your employer has a reimbursement plan but perhaps because of their cash flow problems, you don't request reimbursement for employer expenses you've paid. In this case, *you lose your deduction forever*, since the IRS will not allow you to convert your employer's expenses into a deduction of your own simply because of your lack of action. When reimbursements are general policy but it's a condition of your employment not to receive any, deductions have, on rare occasions, been allowed. The moral: If you're entitled to reimbursement, request it, even if your employer doesn't pay it.

Unreimbursed expenses. Even if you're expected to pay certain expenses as a condition of your employment, deductibility is not assured. There should be a reasonable relationship between the expenditures and your compensation. Get a written statement or corporate resolution which says your compensation plan is based on expecting you to incur various auto and/or other stated expenses. This will indicate to the IRS that it's *necessary* for you to pay such expenses and that the amount of your compensation has been taken into consideration to cover those expenses.

Keep in mind that with good records and whether reimbursed or not, you can deduct any job-related expenses you feel are necessary to do your job. However, they should be primarily for *your* benefit, not your employer's.

Other special situations. If you're related to your employer, all reimbursements, unless you're using the standard mileage rate, must be reported on your tax return as income. (Related means siblings, children, stepchildren, spouses, ancestors, and lineal descendants.)

Basically, the same rules apply if you and/or your relatives own more than 10% of the outstanding stock of the corporation which employs you. Unless you use the 21¢ per mile rate, you must keep records for travel and entertainment expenses and report them on your return. This is also true if an unincorporated employer is a member of your family.

Any personal expenses—travel, meals, and lodging expenses for family members who accompany you on a business trip, for example—that are

subsequently reimbursed to you must be included as income.

Tax$aver Tip. *If you consistently incur expenses and are not reimbursed, discuss with your employer a reduction in salary or commission and replace this decrease with a fixed expense allowance of approximately the same amount. The resultant salary reduction may not only save some payroll taxes but will also help you justify deductions if you're audited.* ■

Automobile Casualty & Theft Losses

Automobile casualty damages or losses that occur when a car is stolen may be deductible. Questions then arise regarding the determination of the amount of the loss and whether the car was used for personal or business purposes, or both.

Generally, business losses are fully deductible, reduced only by any insurance or other reimbursements. Personal casualty or theft losses, on the other hand, are subject to certain reductions and limitations which, in effect, allow only *major* losses to be deductible. In addition, such losses can be claimed *only* if you itemize your deductions.

Keep track of these losses on the form on page 125.

Casualty Losses

The IRS defines casualty as "the damage, destruction, or loss of property resulting from an identifiable event that is sudden, unexpected, or unusual. A sudden event is one that is swift, not gradual or progressive. An unexpected event is

one that is ordinarily unanticipated and one that you do not intend. An unusual event is one that is not a day-to-day occurrence and one that is not typical of the activity in which you were engaged."

What is a casualty loss as it relates to your car? IRS regulations describe it as damage to a car you own, whether used for business or pleasure, when the damage results from the faulty driving of the person operating the automobile but not due to a willful act or willful negligence, or when it results from the faulty driving of the operator of the vehicle with which the taxpayer's car collides.

Business auto casualty losses. These losses are fully deductible after reduction by the amount of insurance or other reimbursements received or expected. If the casualty loss involves a car used only partially for business, the loss must be divided as if there were two separate occurrences.

Generally, a casualty loss amount is the lesser of either the car's adjusted basis at the time the loss occurred or the decrease in the car's fair market value from immediately before to immediately after the casualty. However, if the car is *completely* destroyed, the deductible loss is the adjusted basis less any salvage value or insurance proceeds or other compensation either received or sure to be recovered.

Personal auto casualty losses. As with business losses, the amount of the loss is the value of the destroyed portion of the car or the adjusted basis, whichever is less, reduced by any insurance or other reimbursements received or expected. However, there are two other reductions you must make:

1. Each loss must be reduced by $100.
2. You must further reduce the combined amount of all losses, casualty or theft, by 10% of your adjusted gross income.

The remaining balance is the amount you may claim on your return. These reductions do not apply if you had a casualty gain because reimbursements exceeded your losses.

Married taxpayers filing jointly are subject to only one $100 reduction for each casualty (or theft) loss on their return. But each of them is subject to that limitation if they file separate returns.

Disaster area losses. If your loss is a result of a disaster in an area the President declares eligible for federal assistance, you have an additional option. You can claim the loss either in the year it occurred or in the immediately *preceding* tax year. Consult your tax advisor to find out what's best for your particular situation.

Examples of deductible losses. For your reference, the following events have been allowed as deductions for property losses and damages:

- Accidents, if unavoidable
- Cleanup expenses
- Earthquakes, earthslides, avalanches, sudden sinking of land
- Explosions, bomb damage, fires, lightning
- Hail, snow, icy roads, blizzards, dust storms, hurricanes, tornadoes, sudden wind damage
- Vandalism, looting, riots
- Water rise (if sudden), floods, tidal waves

Examples of nondeductible losses. The IRS has not allowed the following:

- Appraisal or estimator fees
- Cost of unsuccessful auto accident property damage claim
- Erosion, rust, paint oxidation
- Muffler, fuel pump damage by large stones on road*
- Personal injury damages paid, attorney fees, court costs
- Pet damage to auto*
- Progressive deterioration of any type
- Rental of car while own car was being repaired*
- Salt water exposure
- Tire blowout due to overloading*

* May be deductible if related to business or income-producing purposes

Losses from Theft

The theft of a car, an illegal act usually done with criminal intent, is a deductible loss, subject to certain rules and limitations.

When to deduct. Such losses are deductible only in the year of discovery, which may or may not be the year the theft actually took place. If the year of discovery is over and you haven't filed your return yet, don't claim the loss if you think the car will be recovered; deduct such a loss only when it's clear that recovery will not occur. Then you'll need to prove that you were the owner of the car, that it was actually stolen, when you first discovered the theft, and how you arrived at the dollar amount of the loss.

If your car is stolen, contact a law enforcement agency and your insurance company just as soon as you discover the theft. For tax purposes, it's not required that the police actually investigate the theft.

Amount of loss. The cost of the car and its fair market value at the time of the theft must be determined. As a cost basis, use your original sales contract, written proof of the car's cost from the files of the previous owner, or the current value shown in a standard valuation book. For business cars your loss is either the full fair market value or its adjusted basis (original cost plus improvements, less depreciation, even if not claimed), whichever is less. Ignore depreciation for nonbusiness cars. If you later recover your car, your loss is either the decline in value from the time it was stolen until the time recovered or the adjusted basis before the theft, whichever is less.

Each nonbusiness theft loss must be reduced first by any insurance or other reimbursements and second by $100. Then, combine your theft loss with any casualty losses and deduct 10% of your adjusted gross income from Form 1040. This is the net amount you can claim. These reductions do not apply if you had a casualty gain because reimbursements exceeded your losses.

If the car was used only for business, it's not subject to the $100 reduction or the 10% of adjusted gross income reduction, but it must be reduced by any reimbursements.

If, as is often the case, the car was used for both business and personal purposes, treat the theft as if there were two separate occurrences, applying the $100 and 10% rules only to the non-business portion of the loss.

Supporting Your Claim

As you might expect, there have been many court cases involving casualty and theft losses claimed by taxpayers. These cases clearly show that you must have adequate, written evidence to support your claim.

For personal or business losses, use the form provided. In addition, gather the following written information as soon after the loss occurs as possible:

1. A statement as to the nature and type of casualty, and how the loss was a direct result of the casualty, with copies of any available insurance, fire, or police reports

2. Proof of ownership of the car or, if leased, that you were contractually liable for the damage

3. A sales contract, lease agreement, or other evidence supporting the purchase price; receipts and canceled checks to support any major additions or improvements to the car

4. Appraisals, insurance adjustors' opinions, or reports showing how the fair market value (before and after the casualty) was determined (for auto accidents, this is usually a damage estimate by a qualified person)

5. Photographs showing the extent of damage

6. Receipts for any damage repairs completed

7. In a case of theft, a copy of the police report proving the theft and showing when you discovered the car was missing

Many taxpayers do not file insurance claims for casualty and theft losses because they fear that their insurance premiums may increase or that the policy may even be canceled. In such cases, the Tax Reform Act of 1986 says that you are not allowed to claim a nonbusiness casualty loss deduction unless you file a timely insurance claim.

Tax$aver Tip. *It's important, and usually relatively easy, to prove the original purchase price of your car. If you don't, the IRS may use an arbitrary percentage of the amount you paid for it, which could reduce your loss dramatically. If you use a value from a standard valuation book, be sure to add or subtract from the retail value for major accessories, mileage, and overall condition.*

Adjustments to cost basis. All property, business or personal, has an ongoing measurement of investment, called basis, which usually is the original cost. Casualty and theft losses decrease your basis, since you subtract the amount of the deductible loss and any insurance or other reimbursements received. Any money spent to repair or restore your car will increase the basis. And if your reimbursements are greater than the basis before the casualty, this excess is added to the basis.

How and where to report. If your situation involves a wide range of gains and losses involving various types of property or if insurance proceeds exceed the loss, you may have to amend prior years' returns. In this event, consult your tax advisor.

To report casualty or theft losses, transfer the information on page 125 to Form 4684; use Section A for personal casualty and theft losses, Section B for business losses. If the amounts claimed are large, you'd be wise to attach documentation directly to your return. Publications 547, 549, and 584 are available from the IRS if you need more information. ■

Other Deductible Uses of an Automobile

Many expenses for other uses of an automobile, such as for charitable, medical, moving, job-hunting, and educational purposes, are deductible, but only if you itemize your deductions.

Using a Car for Charitable Purposes

At home or away, auto expenses directly related to or for activities benefiting a "qualified" charitable organization are deductible—but only if you itemize—at the current standard mileage rate of 12¢ per mile. Or you may deduct your actual costs of gas and oil. Parking fees and tolls are deductible either way. General repairs and maintenance, insurance, and depreciation are *not* deductible. Record your mileage, gas and oil, and other expenses, less any reimbursements, in the log on page 84. The travel must be exclusively for charitable purposes, according to the provisions of the Tax Reform Act of 1986.

To find out if the organization is qualified, ask the IRS or the organization itself. Generally, the organization has to be operated solely for religious, educational, or other charitable purposes.

Tax$aver Tips. *We suggest you compute your deduction twice, first with the standard mileage rate, then with the actual cost method, and claim the larger amount. If you receive a reimbursement greater than your expenses, you must include the excess in income. But when expenses exceed the reimbursement, deduct only the net amount.*

In some cases, you may not wish to receive a reimbursement from the organization for your expenses. But if you want to deduct your expenses, you should accept the reimbursement and write a check for the same amount to the organization.

Other out-of-pocket expenses. In rendering services to qualified organizations, deductions are allowed for such costs as transportation, meals, and lodging while away from home; uniforms; postage; stationery items; and telephone calls. Not deductible are costs of baby-sitters, meals if not away from home, and trips for meetings of chambers of commerce, international organizations, political parties or candidates, civic and social clubs, and labor unions.

Gifts of property other than cash. If you donate auto equipment or accessories, or even a car, to a qualified organization, the amount deductible generally is limited to the fair market value of the item on the date the donation is made. If your gift is valued at more than $500, you must attach a statement to your return detailing the date, name and address of the organization, description of the property, date and how acquired by you, fair market value and how computed, cost basis if appreciated property, any reductions in value of the appreciated property and how computed, terms of agreement with the organization as to your subsequent use of the property (if any), and the amount you're claiming as a deduction.

Starting in 1985, you must also attach a written qualified appraisal if the claimed deduction exceeds $5,000.

When, how, and where to deduct. Effective in 1987, only people who itemize their deductions may deduct charitable contributions; they must be paid or given before the end of the tax year. Report them on Schedule A, Form 1040. Generally, your deduction is limited to 50% of your adjusted gross income, but some may be limited to 30% or occasionally even to 20%.

Using a Car for Medical & Dental Purposes

The cost of using a car is deductible for itemizers when it's related to the diagnosis, cure, mitigation, treatment, or prevention of disease or for the purpose of affecting any part or function of the body. (Physical and mental disorders, defects, or illnesses are all diseases.)

Trips are deductible if they're related to medical insurance premiums, as are trips to a pharmacy to purchase medicines or drugs but only if prescribed by a doctor.

Record your medical-related trips and expenses (see below) in the log on page 85 and be sure to save receipts and documentation.

Auto expenses. Local and away-from-home travel expenses are deductible at a current standard mileage rate of 9¢ per mile. Or you may deduct your actual costs of gas and oil. Parking fees and tolls are fully deductible. Again, general repairs and maintenance, insurance, and depreciation are *not* deductible. Usually, actual costs will be higher than the 9¢ per mile rate, but it's always wise to compute the expense both ways and claim the larger amount.

The best way to do this is to total your monthly costs of gas and oil and divide by the total mileage for the month. Then multiply by medical miles driven and compare the result with the 9¢ per mile computation. Medical-related transportation by bus, plane, taxi, or train is also deductible.

Cost of away-from-home medical travel is allowed by the IRS if the trip is primarily for medical purposes, not pleasure or personal interests; if the person taking the trip has a specific ailment or condition and was treated previously by someone in a medical capacity; and if the destination helps alleviate or cure the ailment or condition, is temporary, and was advised by a doctor. Meals and lodging en route are deductible but *not* after arrival, unless the taxpayer is hospitalized.

Special auto equipment. You can deduct the cost of hand controls or other special equipment installed for the use of a handicapped person. You may *not*, however, deduct the day-to-day operating cost of a car just because it is so equipped. The purchase price and maintenance cost of an autoette (a small auto for the handicapped) or a wheelchair, if used primarily for the alleviation of sickness or disability (not simply for transportation to work), are allowable medical expenses. If a car is designed or modified to carry a wheelchair, the *extra* cost only is deductible as a medical expense.

Medical or business expense? If you're unsure how to categorize an expense, deduct it as an employee business expense if it meets all of the following criteria:

1. It's needed essentially for you to do your work satisfactorily.

2. It's for goods and services not ordinarily needed or used in personal activities.
3. It's not covered by medical deduction rules.

When, how, and where to deduct. Expenses actually paid before the end of the tax year are claimed as itemized deductions on Schedule A, Form 1040. Be sure to reduce your deductions by the amount of any insurance or other reimbursements received during the tax year. Only the excess medical expenses which exceed 7½% (effective in 1987) of adjusted gross income are allowable as a deduction. You may deduct medical expenses for yourself, your spouse, and your dependents.

For a list of deductible and nondeductible medical expenses, ask for IRS Publication 502.

Tax$aver Tip. *If you or your spouse had unusually high medical expenses, you may save taxes by filing separate returns. Compute the taxes both ways, jointly and separately, and file the return which results in the lowest amount of tax.*

Using a Car for Moving Purposes

Employees and self-employed persons can deduct job-related moving expenses. It doesn't matter if you're transferred by your employer or you quit and found a new job on your own. Self-employed people must move for legitimate business reasons to qualify for the deduction. Though there are numerous tests and requirements to be met, we'll discuss only the *time* and *distance* tests here.

The *time* test for employees means that you must work full time at least 39 weeks during the first 12 months after arriving at the new job location. Self-employed people must work full time at least 78 weeks during the first 24 months after arrival. The *distance* test states that your new principal place of employment must be at least 35 miles farther from your former residence than was your former principal place of work, or if you had no former principal place of work, it must be at least 35 miles from your former residence. Others who can claim moving expenses are high school and college graduates seeking new employment and people re-entering the work force after a period of unemployment.

Deductible auto use. There are three types of deductible automobile moving expenses. First are the house-hunting trips before you actually move. You can deduct travel, meals, and lodging while you're traveling to and from the new area and also while you're there. However, to be deductible, such trips must take place *after* you've obtained a job in the new area and must be primarily for the purpose of finding a new place to live. If you're self-employed, you also must have made "substantial" arrangements (determined by the IRS on a case-by-case basis) to begin work at the new location. Your attempts to find a new residence need not be successful for the expense to be deductible, and there is no limit on the number of trips you or the members of your household may make.

Second, if you rent a trailer to move household goods and personal items to your new home, the costs of transportation, meals, and lodging for your entire household, plus the cost of the trailer, are deductible. You can deduct such expenses beginning the day before you actually leave, during the entire time en route, and on the day you arrive. Only one trip is deductible.

Third, the above paragraph applies if you're simply driving to your new location while your household goods are being shipped separately. Also, you can deduct the cost of shipping cars and household pets. Though you can deduct living expenses, including meals and lodging, for a 30-day period after you move *if* you're in temporary quarters, there's no further deduction for auto use as a moving expense during the same 30 days.

Record keeping. Record your auto mileage and expenses in the log on page 87. Note that in order to complete Form 3903, you'll need to keep premove mileage and expenses separate from those incurred on the move itself. Keeping a daily diary of all moving-related activities will provide added substantiation. Save receipts and other documentation since estimates are not acceptable.

When, how, and where to deduct. The IRS allows two methods to compute moving-related auto expenses. You can either use the standard 9¢ per mile rate, plus parking and tolls, or deduct your actual costs of gas, oil, parking, tolls, and repairs (occurring on the trip). The actual cost method

59

usually results in the larger deduction. No deductions are allowed for depreciation, insurance, or repairs resulting from an accident.

You may claim these expenses on Form 3903 either in the year you incurred the expenses or in the year you paid them. Effective in 1987, moving expenses are deducted on Schedule A as an itemized deduction, both for the self-employed and employees. Reimbursements from employers should be reported as income in the year received on Form 1040.

If you deduct the expenses and later don't meet the time test, you can either amend the prior return, eliminating that deduction and paying additional tax, or you can simply include the total amount of your previously claimed moving expense deduction in other income on Form 1040 in the year you fail to meet the test.

There is no limitation on the costs of travel and moving your household goods to your new home, but the combined total of all other moving expenses can't exceed $3,000. Also, your combined deduction for pre-move house-hunting trips and living expenses is limited to $1,500. If married and filing separately, you're limited to half the above amounts. For details, see IRS Publication 521.

Using a Car for Job-Hunting Purposes

Here's a list of deductible and nondeductible situations when you use a car to find a new job.

The following are deductible auto expenses:

- You look for a *new* job in your *current* occupation, whether you're successful or not.
- You're unemployed and are looking for the *same* kind of work you did for your last employer, but only if a substantial amount of time has not passed.
- You travel to and from a new area to look for a job in your present occupation, but only if the primary purpose of the trip is to look for the job.
- You travel looking for a job while in the new area, even though the cost of getting there and back is not deductible due to the primary purpose rule above.
- You use your car to visit employment agencies and have resumés prepared or distributed.

The following are *not* deductible auto expenses:

- You look for a job in a new occupation and are successful.

- There's a substantial period of time that you were unemployed and looking for a job.
- You're looking for employment for the first time, even if you're successful.
- You travel to a new area to look for a job, but the primary purpose of the trip is personal or pleasure.

You may use either the standard mileage rate (21¢) or the actual cost method to compute your deduction. Record your mileage and expenses in the log on page 86. (If you need more space, use a blank column in one of the mileage logs and/or in the Automobile Expense Register.) Claim the deduction, subject to a floor of 2% of adjusted gross income, on Schedule A.

Using a Car for Educational Purposes

The use of your car for educational purposes is deductible only if the cost of your educational expenses is deductible. To determine this, consult your tax advisor. If you meet the tests, you're allowed to deduct the following travel expenses:

1. Between your general work area and a school located beyond that area

2. Between where you work and a school within the same general area

3. Between your home and school if it's not farther than if you traveled from work to school

To determine your deduction, you can choose either the standard mileage rate (21¢) or the actual cost method. Keep track of your mileage and expenses in the log on page 86. (If you need more space, use a blank column in one of the mileage logs and/or in the Automobile Expense Register.) On a day you don't work, you can't deduct the cost to get from home to school, since this is considered a commuting expense. Claim educational expenses on Schedule A as a miscellaneous deduction, subject to a floor of 2% of adjusted gross income.

For more information about educational expenses, request IRS Publication 508. ■

Logs & Registers

The various logs and registers you'll need to keep track of your mileage and expenses throughout the year, as well as how to determine and claim your deduction, are explained on the following pages.

Using the Mileage Logs

The mileage logs described below will help you record, compute, and document the following important figures:

- Total miles driven for all uses
- Total miles driven for business purposes
- Percentage of business use
- Average daily round-trip commuting distance
- Total miles driven for commuting
- Other personal mileage

Other mileage logs you may need for specific purposes are explained in the section beginning on page 55.

To total your mileage for the year, use the form called Summary of All Miles Driven on page 87.

Permanent Recurring Mileage Record (page 72). Use this form to reduce the time you spend entering odometer readings for trips (including those away from home) you make on a regular basis, even your daily commute. Simply record the odometer readings one time, note the location and purpose, and check one way or round-trip. Then assign a code, such as A, B, etc., to each trip. For subsequent trips, just use the recurring trip log.

Log of Recurring Trips (page 73). Record recurring trips in this log, using the information from the permanent record. When recording the dates, choose a time period that's most suitable for the particular trip. Or enter the beginning date and wait until the space is filled before entering the ending date; then just start over on a new line.

In the column "Ongoing Count or Dates," enter either a mark for each trip for this code or just the date. Enter the total number of trips for that period in the next column. Then simply multiply by the number of miles to arrive at a total and distribute the total in the proper column.

Log of Nonrecurring Trips (page 78). Use this log for nonregular auto use, entering the information for each trip, even those away from home. Though you can maintain this log on a weekly basis, you'll need to keep track of the date, destination, and odometer readings for each trip as it occurs.

Sampling: A New Time-Saving Technique

As an alternative to keeping your logs on a daily or weekly basis, the IRS has approved a sampling method for taxpayers whose auto use is regular. The logic is this: if you maintain adequate, detailed records for only *part* of a tax year and can prove by other evidence that the period you chose is *typical* of your annual auto use, the business use percentage so established can be used without your having to keep year-long records.

Though you can choose your own sampling period, the IRS has made two suggestions:

1. Keep records for the first 3 months, determine your percentage, and use it for the year.

2. Maintain adequate records during the first week of every month.

Though the business use percentage in the second example won't be the same each month, it's assumed, though not yet clarified by the IRS, you'd simply average them and use that percentage for the entire year.

If you're using the sampling method, be sure you can prove that the periods chosen are representative of the rest of the year. Don't use it if your auto travel for business is unpredictable from day to day or week to week. Also, you can't use any sampling method if you drive your employer's car and it's available for use by any other employee for all or even part of the year.

Using the Expense Logs

This section explains how and where to record your automobile expenses for the year, regardlesss of the method you use to compute your deduction.

Automobile Expense Register (page 88). This register is primarily designed for use with the actual cost method (see page 20), since you must keep detailed records of all auto expenses for the year. But even if you choose the standard mileage rate method, you can use this register to record parking fees, interest payments, and, where applicable, personal property tax. Enter your expenses on a regular basis, being sure to stay up to date. Then transfer your monthly totals to the annual summary on page 112.

For each payment by check, simply list the date, who was paid, a brief description of what the check was for, and the check number. If you have large and frequent business expenses, it's wise to maintain a separate checking account for all auto-related expenses. Then, when you reconcile the account each month, you can quickly record in the expense register all your auto expenses for that period.

For payments by credit card, simply enter "CC" in the proper column when each expense is incurred. Or you can wait until you receive your monthly credit card statement, write one check, and distribute the expenses to the proper columns on the register. This will also save some space on the register to record other expenses.

Tax$aver Tip. *Tax law allows you to deduct credit card charges in the year **incurred**, even if the actual payment occurs in the following year.*

For payments made in cash, be sure to get receipts if at all possible and record the expenditures as soon as you can. A method of keeping track of these cash expenditures in your checkbook is explained under "Self-Reimbursement Form for Expenses Paid in Cash," page 67.

Under the column "Equipment Additions," record any permanent additions with a useful life of more than a year or improvements which either increase the value of your car or prolong its useful life. Transfer all equipment additions to page 71 so that all depreciable assets, past and present, are recorded in one place.

For payments that don't fit the column headings provided, label and use blank columns for frequently made payments and the "Miscellaneous Expenses" column for nonrecurring ones.

65

Tax$aver Tips. *Ask for receipts for all your expenditures and store them in one place, perhaps an envelope you keep in your car.*

If you have bills due for car expenses at the end of the year, pay them before year-end (except for credit card charges); otherwise, they won't be deductible until the following year.

Don't claim large amounts on your return for categories such as miscellaneous or other expenses. It's always best to identify large amounts separately and show miscellaneous or other expenses as smaller amounts.

Away-from-Home Business Expense Log (page 114).

Out-of-pocket expenses incurred away from home and related to your trade, business, or investment activities are deductible, but only if you're away for more than a day. (Investment-related expenses must be directly attributable to income-producing activity, as explained on page 44.) In order to establish that the trip was an ordinary and neces-sary business expense, you'll need to indicate the date of departure and return, the business pur-pose, and the mileage on one of the mileage logs. Starting in 1987, you can only deduct 80% of the cost of business meals and entertainment. If you eat alone, the entire cost is deductible.

Record in the log each day's expenses as they occur. Transfer all subtotals to the top of the follow-ing log page. (For information on how to handle reimbursements, see page 46.)

To fully substantiate away-from-home business expenses, you must also obtain and save receipts, itemized bills or statements, canceled checks, and other such documentary evidence for all lodging, regardless of the amount, and for other expen-ditures of $25 or more (not including tips), except for transportation when a receipt is not readily available.

Automobile Business Entertainment Expense Log (page 123). Record your business entertainment expenses in this log. To arrive at the cost of using your car, multiply the total mileage for each trip by 21¢ per mile and enter the amount under "Auto Use." When you're preparing your return, simply

add the totals to your non-automobile entertainment expenses to arrive at your total business entertainment deduction.

Self-Reimbursement Form for Expenses Paid in Cash (page 126). Here you can periodically summarize typical out-of-pocket expenses paid in cash (use a diary or tape recorder to accumulate them and always get receipts when possible). In order to have all your expenses recorded by check, write a check to yourself for the total you recorded from the same bank account you use to pay your other business expenses. You can then record the check in the Automobile Expense Register, filling in the appropriate columns. Keep all receipts that relate to each check together.

Reimbursements Received from Others (page 128). All expense reimbursements received during the year should be recorded on this form.

Automobile Deduction Checklist

The following list summarizes deductible automobile expenditures. Refer to it often to be sure you're not overlooking any deductible expenses.

Deductible Whether Related to Business or Pleasure
Casualty and theft losses
Charitable miles driven
Interest on auto loan or gas credit card
    (nonbusiness portion to be phased out)
License fees (if treated as personal property tax)
Medical coverage in auto insurance
Medical miles driven

Deductible Only as Related to Business Use
Air conditioners*
Alarm systems*, theft prevention kits
Alternators, generators
Auto club membership fees and dues
Auto repair books and manuals, maps
Batteries, testers, chargers, booster cables
Brakes, repairs, parts
Carburetors, parts, kits
Carpets, floor mats, upholstery
Car rental fees, taxi fares
Chauffeurs' salaries and licenses
Convertible tops*, boots*, sunroofs*, covers
Damages from faulty driving
Depreciation
Educational miles driven

Emergency repair kits, road lights, safety flares, safety belts

Fan belts, hoses

Gas, oil, lubes

Headlights, lamps, spotlights, fog lights, flashlights, mirrors

Installation costs*

Insurance, license and registration fees

Interest on auto loan or gas credit card

Investment and production of income miles

Job-hunting miles driven

Keys, key chains

Lease payments

Loss on sale of car

Luggage racks and carriers*

Moving expense miles driven

Muffler parts and repairs, shock absorbers

Oil, changes, filters, pans

Parking fees and meters, garage rental, tolls

Radiator cleaning and flushing, antifreeze

Radios*, stereos*, speakers*, tape players*, CB antennas, cellular phones*, clocks

Rebuilt engines*

Repairs, maintenance, tools

Smog and diagnostic inspections

Sparkplugs, tune-up kits

Starters, voltage regulators

Tax$aver

Tires*, hubcaps, chains, jacks

Tow bars*, roll bars*

Valve adjustment and parts

Wash, wax, polish, cleaners, applicators

Windshield washers, fluids, wiper arms and blades

Wire wheels*, mags*, rims, wheel balancing and alignment

* May have to depreciate

Determining Your Total Deduction for the Year

Forms in this book allow you to compute your total automobile deduction for the year, whether you use the standard mileage rate or the actual cost method. (You may want to attach a copy of the completed form to your tax return.)

Standard mileage rate. Compute your deduction on the form on page 129. Note that the business use percentage includes investment miles driven in order to compute your partially deductible interest and property tax expenses. To determine if you meet the 50% test, use lines (A), (B), and (C) at the top of the form on page 130 to compute the percentage. Remember that you're not allowed to include any investment miles you drove to see if you meet the 50% test.

Actual cost method. Use the form on page 130 to compute the two business use percentages and your total deduction for the year.

Expenses you should claim separately. Be aware that your total auto deduction for business/investment use, no matter what method you're using, does *not* include the following, all of which must be claimed separately: auto use for business entertainment, casualty and theft losses, charitable miles driven, educational expense travel, job-hunting miles driven, medical miles driven, and travel expenses for moving. Away-from-home business expenses should also be claimed separately, though auto use connected with these expenses is included in your total deduction.

Claiming Deductions on Your Return

Where taxpayers claim deductible automobile expenses on their tax return depends on their income-earning status.

Employees and *outside salespeople* report their expenses on Form 2106. Effective in 1987, *both* deduct any expenses that exceed reimbursements as a miscellaneous deduction on Schedule A; this deduction is limited to the amount that exceeds 2% of adjusted gross income.

Self-employed people who are sole owners of a business use Schedule C, Form 1040—Profit or (Loss) From Business or Profession. If there's more than one owner, use Form 1065 for partnerships and Form 1120 if incorporated.

Investors who invest primarily in securities deduct auto expenses on Schedule A. Effective in 1987, this deduction is subject to the 2% floor. Investors who receive rental or royalty income deduct related auto and travel expenses on Schedule E. ∎

Record of Important Information & Dates

Personal Information

Name_____ Address _____

City _____ State _____ Zip _____

Telephone: Home _____ Business _____

Automobile Information

Odometer Reading Jan. 1, 19____: _____ Dec. 31, 19____: _____

Year & Make_____ Model_____

Vehicle ID No. _____ Vehicle Weight_____ Lbs.

Engine Serial No. _____ Color _____

Recommended Fuel _____ Oil Weight & Grade _____

Tire Size _____ Recommended Pressure _____

Capacities: Coolant _____

    Fuel _____ Oil/Filter No. _____

    Transmission _____ Radiator _____

Licensing Information

State License Plate No. _____

State Driver's License No. _____

Oil Company Credit Card Information

Card Issued by	Account Number	Expiration Date

Insurance Information

Company_____ Telephone _____

Agent _____ Telephone _____

Policy Number_____ Annual Premium _____

Loss Payable Clause to _____

Type of Insurance

Liability		Collision & Comprehensive	
Coverage	Limits	Coverage	Limits

Important Dates

Description	Expiration Date or Payment Due
Automobile Insurance Policy	
State Licensing Fees	
State Automobile Registration	
State Property Tax	
State Driver's License	
Automobile Club Membership Dues	
Automobile Lease Agreement	

Automobile Cost, Basis & Depreciation Information

Date Acq'd. or Placed in Service	Mileage at Start	Description of Automobile & Major Additions	Cost			Basis Adjust-ments Sec. 179 or ITC (B)	Cost Basis for Depreciation (A) Less (B)	Depreciation				
			Unrecov-ered Cost of Trade-in	Cash Paid or Financed	Total Cost (A)			Class	Method	%	Unrecov-ered Cost at Start of Year	Depreci-ation This Year

Note: This form is designed for use by you or your tax advisor for reference and tax-planning purposes. Investment tax credit claimed on autos before 1986 may be subject to recapture when auto is sold or traded. Depreciation computed on form is subject to certain limitations and may be further reduced by application of business use percentage. Transfer information to next year's book. For more information, see page 26.

Permanent Recurring Mileage Record

Code	From/to & Business Purpose or Benefit Expected or Received	Odometer			Check		Code	From/to & Business Purpose or Benefit Expected or Received	Odometer			Check	
		Depart	Arrive	Miles Each Trip	One Way	R/T			Depart	Arrive	Miles Each Trip	One Way	R/T
A	Home to office commute	9,086	9,138	26	✓								
B	Office to XYZ Co. customer	10,641	10,715	74		✓							

Log of Recurring Trips

Inclusive Dates	Code	Miles Each Trip (A)	Number of Trips in Period		Miles Driven (A) × (B)	Trade or Business	Investment	Entertain- ment	Commuting		
			Ongoing Count or Dates	Total(B)							
1/1 to 1/31	A	26	ᵀᴴᴴ ᵀᴴᴴ III	13	338				338		
1/1 to 1/15	B	74	1/5, 1/7, 1/9, 1/10, 1/12, 1/14	6	444	444					
to											
to											
to											
to											
to											
to											
to											
to											
to											
to											
to											
to											
to											
Note: See page 63 for instructions.		Subtotals									

73

Log of Recurring Trips

Inclusive Dates	Total Repeat Mileage for Period						Distribution of Miles Driven in Period					
	Code	Miles Each Trip (A)	Number of Trips in Period		Miles Driven (A) × (B)	Trade or Business	Investment	Entertain-ment	Commuting		
			Ongoing Count or Dates	Total(B)							
to											
to											
to											
to											
to											
to											
to											
to											
to											
to											
to											
to											
to											
to											
to											
Note: See page 63 for instructions.	Subtotals										

74

Log of Recurring Trips

Inclusive Dates	Total Repeat Mileage for Period					Distribution of Miles Driven in Period					
	Code	Miles Each Trip (A)	Number of Trips in Period		Miles Driven (A) × (B)	Trade or Business	Investment	Entertain-ment	Commuting		
			Ongoing Count or Dates	Total(B)							
to											
to											
to											
to											
to											
to											
to											
to											
to											
to											
to											
to											
to											
to											
to											
Note: See page 63 for instructions.	Subtotals										

75

Log of Recurring Trips

Inclusive Dates	Total Repeat Mileage for Period					Distribution of Miles Driven in Period					
	Code	Miles Each Trip (A)	Number of Trips in Period		Miles Driven (A) × (B)	Trade or Business	Investment	Entertainment	Commuting		
			Ongoing Count or Dates	Total(B)							
to											
to											
to											
to											
to											
to											
to											
to											
to											
to											
to											
to											
to											
to											
to											
Note: See page 63 for instructions.		Subtotals									

Log of Recurring Trips

Inclusive Dates	Total Repeat Mileage for Period					Distribution of Miles Driven in Period					
	Code	Miles Each Trip (A)	Number of Trips in Period		Miles Driven (A) × (B)	Trade or Business	Investment	Entertain-ment	Commuting		
			Ongoing Count or Dates	Total(B)							
to											
to											
to											
to											
to											
to											
to											
to											
to											
to											
to											
to											
to											
to											
to											
Note: See page 63 for instructions.	**Totals for Year**										

Log of Nonrecurring Trips

Date 19 __	From/to	Business Purpose or Benefit Expected or Received	Odometer			Details of Miles Driven					
			Depart	Arrive	Miles This Trip	Trade or Business	Invest-ment	Enter-tainment			
1/6	Office to Bishop Co. R/T	Prospective customer referred by XYZ Co.	10,778	10,862	84	84					
1/7	Office to Plaza R/T	dinner with R.J. Little, prev. TPI, re product	10,981	10,928	18			18			
Note: Odometer readings are sufficient for round-trips but are not necessary for in-between stops. See page 64 for instructions.			Subtotals								

Log of Nonrecurring Trips

Date 19 __	From/to	Business Purpose or Benefit Expected or Received	Odometer			Details of Miles Driven					
			Depart	Arrive	Miles This Trip	Trade or Business	Invest-ment	Enter-tainment			
Note: Odometer readings are sufficient for round-trips but are not necessary for in-between stops. See page 64 for instructions.		Subtotals									

Log of Nonrecurring Trips

Date 19 __	From/to	Business Purpose or Benefit Expected or Received	Odometer			Details of Miles Driven					
			Depart	Arrive	Miles This Trip	Trade or Business	Invest-ment	Enter-tainment			
Note: Odometer readings are sufficient for round-trips but are not necessary for in-between stops. See page 64 for instructions.		Subtotals									

Log of Nonrecurring Trips

Date 19 __	From/to	Business Purpose or Benefit Expected or Received	Odometer			Details of Miles Driven					
			Depart	Arrive	Miles This Trip	Trade or Business	Invest-ment	Enter-tainment			
Note: Odometer readings are sufficient for round-trips but are not necessary for in-between stops. See page 64 for instructions.		Subtotals									

Log of Nonrecurring Trips

Date 19 __	From/to	Business Purpose or Benefit Expected or Received	Odometer			Details of Miles Driven					
			Depart	Arrive	Miles This Trip	Trade or Business	Invest-ment	Enter-tainment			
Note: Odometer readings are sufficient for round-trips but are not necessary for in-between stops. See page 64 for instructions.		Subtotals									

82

Log of Nonrecurring Trips

Date 19 __	From/to	Business Purpose or Benefit Expected or Received	Odometer			Details of Miles Driven					
			Depart	Arrive	Miles This Trip	Trade or Business	Invest-ment	Enter-tainment			
Note: Odometer readings are sufficient for round-trips but are not necessary for in-between stops. See page 64 for instructions.		Totals for Year									

Log of Deductible Auto Use for Charity Purposes

Date 19__	Destination & Reason for Trip	Standard Mileage Rate Method					Parking Fees & Tolls	Actual Expenses				Reimburse-ments
		Odometer		Computation				Gas & Oil	Lodging			
		Start	End	Miles	Rate	Cost						
					× 12¢							
					× 12¢							
					× 12¢							
					× 12¢							
					× 12¢							
					× 12¢							
					× 12¢							
					× 12¢							
					× 12¢							
					× 12¢							
					× 12¢							
					× 12¢							
					× 12¢							
					× 12¢							
					× 12¢							
Note: Transfer totals directly to Schedule A. For more information, see page 55.	**Totals for Year**				× 12¢							

84

Log of Deductible Auto Use for Medical & Dental Purposes

Date 19 __	Destination & Reason for Trip	Standard Mileage Rate Method					Parking Fees & Tolls	Actual Expenses					Reimburse-ments
		Odometer		Computation				Gas & Oil	Lodging				
		Start	End	Miles	Rate	Cost							
					× 9¢								
					× 9¢								
					× 9¢								
					× 9¢								
					× 9¢								
					× 9¢								
					× 9¢								
					× 9¢								
					× 9¢								
					× 9¢								
					× 9¢								
					× 9¢								
					× 9¢								
					× 9¢								
					× 9¢								
Note: Transfer totals directly to Schedule A. For more information, see page 56.		Totals for Year			× 9¢								

85

Log of Deductible Auto Use for Job-Hunting Purposes

Date 19 __	Destination & Reason for Trip	Standard Mileage Rate Method					Parking Fees & Tolls	Actual Expenses				Reimburse-ments
		Odometer		Computation				Gas & Oil	Meals	Lodging		
		Start	End	Miles	Rate	Cost						
					× 21¢							
					× 21¢							
					× 21¢							
					× 21¢							
					× 21¢							
					× 21¢							

Log of Deductible Auto Use for Educational Purposes

Date 19 __	Destination & Reason for Trip	Standard Mileage Rate Method					Parking Fees & Tolls	Actual Expenses				Reimburse-ments
		Odometer		Computation				Gas & Oil				
		Start	End	Miles	Rate	Cost						
					× 21¢							
					× 21¢							
					× 21¢							
					× 21¢							
					× 21¢							
					× 21¢							

Log of Deductible Auto Use for Moving Travel Purposes

| Date 19 __ | Destination & Reason for Trip | Standard Mileage Rate Method | | | | | Parking Fees & Tolls | Actual Expenses | | | | Reimburse-ments |
| | | Odometer | | Computation | | | | Gas & Oil | Meals | Lodging | | |
		Start	End	Miles	Rate	Cost						
					× 9¢							
					× 9¢							
					× 9¢							
					× 9¢							
					× 9¢							
					× 9¢							
					× 9¢							
					× 9¢							

Summary of All Miles Driven for Year 19____

| Log Used | Total Miles for Year | Miles for Uses during Year | | | | | | | | | | |
		Trade or Business	Invest-ment	Enter-tainment	Moving Expenses	Job-hunting	Educa-tional	Medical	Chari-table	Com-muting	Other Personal	
Log of Recurring Trips												
Log of Nonrecurring Trips												
Other Mileage Logs												
Totals for Year												

Automobile Expense Register for Month of _____ 19____

Date 19 __	Paid to/Description	Check #, Cr. Card, or Cash	Gas	Oil	Lube	Wash & Wax	Repairs & Maint.	Tires & Batteries	Other Supplies	Insurance	Taxes	Licenses
1/8	Quick Gas	185	8 41	7 10	5 50	8 00			12 62			
1/19	Cash	186	22 66	2 25		3 00	18 61		4 67			
Note: See page 64 for instructions.		Subtotals										

Loan Payments		Garage Rent	Auto Club Dues	Parking Fees	Tolls							Equipment Additions			Miscellaneous Expenses	
Principal	Interest											Description	New/Used	Amount	Description	Amount
				6 50	8 00										Phone calls	11 40
												Note: Record these additions on page 71.			Subtotals	

89

Automobile Expense Register for Month of _____ 19 ____

Date 19 __	Paid to/Description	Check #, Cr. Card, or Cash	Gas	Oil	Lube	Wash & Wax	Repairs & Maint.	Tires & Batteries	Other Supplies	Insurance	Taxes	Licenses
Note: See page 64 for instructions.		Subtotals										

Loan Payments		Garage Rent	Auto Club Dues	Parking Fees	Tolls						Equipment Additions			Miscellaneous Expenses	
Principal	Interest										Description	New/Used	Amount	Description	Amount
											Note: Record these additions on page 71.			Subtotals	

Automobile Expense Register for Month of _____ 19 ___

Date 19 __	Paid to/Description	Check #, Cr. Card, or Cash	Gas	Oil	Lube	Wash & Wax	Repairs & Maint.	Tires & Batteries	Other Supplies	Insurance	Taxes	Licenses
Note: See page 64 for instructions.		**Subtotals**										

| Loan Payments | | Garage Rent | Auto Club Dues | Parking Fees | Tolls | | | | | Equipment Additions | | | Miscellaneous Expenses | |
Principal	Interest									Description	New/ Used	Amount	Description	Amount
										Note: Record these additions on page 71.			**Subtotals**	

93

Automobile Expense Register for Month of _____ 19 ___

Date 19 __	Paid to/Description	Check #, Cr. Card, or Cash	Gas	Oil	Lube	Wash & Wax	Repairs & Maint.	Tires & Batteries	Other Supplies	Insurance	Taxes	Licenses
Note: See page 64 for instructions.		**Subtotals**										

94

Loan Payments		Garage Rent	Auto Club Dues	Parking Fees	Tolls					Equipment Additions			Miscellaneous Expenses	
Principal	Interest									Description	New/Used	Amount	Description	Amount
										Note: Record these additions on page 71.			**Subtotals**	

Automobile Expense Register for Month of _____ 19____

Date 19 __	Paid to/Description	Check #, Cr. Card, or Cash	Gas	Oil	Lube	Wash & Wax	Repairs & Maint.	Tires & Batteries	Other Supplies	Insurance	Taxes	Licenses
Note: See page 64 for instructions.	Subtotals											

Loan Payments		Garage Rent	Auto Club Dues	Parking Fees	Tolls						Equipment Additions			Miscellaneous Expenses	
Principal	Interest										Description	New/Used	Amount	Description	Amount
											Note: Record these additions on page 71.			**Subtotals**	

Automobile Expense Register for Month of _____ 19____

Date 19 __	Paid to/Description	Check #, Cr. Card, or Cash	Gas	Oil	Lube	Wash & Wax	Repairs & Maint.	Tires & Batteries	Other Supplies	Insurance	Taxes	Licenses
Note: See page 64 for instructions.		**Subtotals**										

Loan Payments		Garage Rent	Auto Club Dues	Parking Fees	Tolls					Equipment Additions			Miscellaneous Expenses	
Principal	Interest									Description	New/Used	Amount	Description	Amount
										Note: Record these additions on page 71.			Subtotals	

Automobile Expense Register for Month of _____ 19 ___

Date 19 __	Paid to/Description	Check #, Cr. Card, or Cash	Gas	Oil	Lube	Wash & Wax	Repairs & Maint.	Tires & Batteries	Other Supplies	Insurance	Taxes	Licenses
Note: See page 64 for instructions.		**Subtotals**										

100

Loan Payments		Garage Rent	Auto Club Dues	Parking Fees	Tolls					Equipment Additions			Miscellaneous Expenses	
Principal	Interest									Description	New/Used	Amount	Description	Amount
									Note: Record these additions on page 71.			Subtotals	

Automobile Expense Register for Month of _____ 19____

Date 19 __	Paid to/Description	Check #, Cr. Card, or Cash	Gas	Oil	Lube	Wash & Wax	Repairs & Maint.	Tires & Batteries	Other Supplies	Insurance	Taxes	Licenses
Note: See page 64 for instructions.		Subtotals										

Loan Payments		Garage Rent	Auto Club Dues	Parking Fees	Tolls					Equipment Additions			Miscellaneous Expenses	
Principal	Interest									Description	New/Used	Amount	Description	Amount
									Note: Record these additions on page 71.			Subtotals	

Automobile Expense Register for Month of _____ 19 ___

Date 19 __	Paid to/Description	Check #, Cr. Card, or Cash	Gas	Oil	Lube	Wash & Wax	Repairs & Maint.	Tires & Batteries	Other Supplies	Insurance	Taxes	Licenses
Note: See page 64 for instructions.		**Subtotals**										

104

Loan Payments		Garage Rent	Auto Club Dues	Parking Fees	Tolls					Equipment Additions			Miscellaneous Expenses	
Principal	Interest									Description	New/Used	Amount	Description	Amount
										Note: Record these additions on page 71.			Subtotals	

Automobile Expense Register for Month of _____ 19____

Date 19 __	Paid to/Description	Check #, Cr. Card, or Cash	Gas	Oil	Lube	Wash & Wax	Repairs & Maint.	Tires & Batteries	Other Supplies	Insurance	Taxes	Licenses
Note: See page 64 for instructions.		**Subtotals**										

Loan Payments		Garage Rent	Auto Club Dues	Parking Fees	Tolls					Equipment Additions			Miscellaneous Expenses	
Principal	Interest									Description	New/Used	Amount	Description	Amount
										Note: Record these additions on page 71.			Subtotals	

Automobile Expense Register for Month of _____ 19____

Date 19 __	Paid to/Description	Check #, Cr. Card, or Cash	Gas	Oil	Lube	Wash & Wax	Repairs & Maint.	Tires & Batteries	Other Supplies	Insurance	Taxes	Licenses
Note: See page 64 for instructions.		**Subtotals**										

108

Loan Payments		Garage Rent	Auto Club Dues	Parking Fees	Tolls							Equipment Additions			Miscellaneous Expenses	
Principal	Interest											Description	New/Used	Amount	Description	Amount
												Note: Record these additions on page 71.			Subtotals	

Automobile Expense Register for Month of _____ 19 ___

Date 19 __	Paid to/Description	Check #, Cr. Card, or Cash	Gas		Oil		Lube		Wash & Wax		Repairs & Maint.		Tires & Batteries		Other Supplies		Insurance		Taxes		Licenses	
Note: See page 64 for instructions.		**Subtotals**																					

Loan Payments		Garage Rent	Auto Club Dues	Parking Fees	Tolls					Equipment Additions			Miscellaneous Expenses	
Principal	Interest									Description	New/Used	Amount	Description	Amount
										Note: Record these additions on page 71.			Subtotals	

Annual Summary of Automobile Expense Register for 19____

Month	Gas	Oil	Lube	Wash & Wax	Repairs & Maint.	Tires & Batteries	Other Supplies	Insurance	Taxes
January									
February									
March									
April									
May									
June									
July									
August									
September									
October									
November									
December									
Totals for Year									

Licenses		Loan Payments		Garage Rent	Auto Club Dues	Parking Fees	Tolls					Equipment Add'ns.		Miscellaneous Expenses		Monthly Totals
		Principal	Interest									New	Used			

Away-from-Home Business Expense Log

Date 19__	City	Auto Rental		Gas & Oil		Parking & Tolls		Bus & Taxi		Lodging		Break-fast		Lunch		Dinner		Enter-tainment		Phone Calls		Travel				Daily Totals	
1/19	LA ret'd. 1/20	63	60	12	72	6	75	—		92	81	6	27	27	12	46	48	44	00	1	80	98	00			399	55
1/27	SD ret'd. 1/28	—		—		—		18	20	65	30	—		10	40	32	85	—			40	88	00			215	15
	Subtotals																										

Away-from-Home Business Expense Log

Date 19__	City	Auto Rental	Gas & Oil	Parking & Tolls	Bus & Taxi	Lodging	Break-fast	Lunch	Dinner	Enter-tainment	Phone Calls			Daily Totals	
	Subtotals														

Away-from-Home Business Expense Log

Date 19__	City	Auto Rental	Gas & Oil	Parking & Tolls	Bus & Taxi	Lodging	Break-fast	Lunch	Dinner	Enter-tainment	Phone Calls			Daily Totals
	Subtotals													

Away-from-Home Business Expense Log

Date 19 __	City	Auto Rental	Gas & Oil	Parking & Tolls	Bus & Taxi	Lodging	Break-fast	Lunch	Dinner	Enter-tainment	Phone Calls			Daily Totals
	Subtotals													

Away-from-Home Business Expense Log

Date 19__	City	Auto Rental	Gas & Oil	Parking & Tolls	Bus & Taxi	Lodging	Break-fast	Lunch	Dinner	Enter-tainment	Phone Calls			Daily Totals
	Subtotals													

Away-from-Home Business Expense Log

Date 19___	City	Auto Rental	Gas & Oil	Parking & Tolls	Bus & Taxi	Lodging	Break-fast	Lunch	Dinner	Enter-tainment	Phone Calls			Daily Totals
Subtotals														

Away-from-Home Business Expense Log

Date 19___	City	Auto Rental	Gas & Oil	Parking & Tolls	Bus & Taxi	Lodging	Break-fast	Lunch	Dinner	Enter-tainment	Phone Calls			Daily Totals
	Subtotals													

Away-from-Home Business Expense Log

Date 19__	City	Auto Rental	Gas & Oil	Parking & Tolls	Bus & Taxi	Lodging	Break-fast	Lunch	Dinner	Enter-tainment	Phone Calls			Daily Totals
	Subtotals													

Away-from-Home Business Expense Log

Date 19__	City	Auto Rental	Gas & Oil	Parking & Tolls	Bus & Taxi	Lodging	Break-fast	Lunch	Dinner	Enter-tainment	Phone Calls			Daily Totals
	Totals for Year													

Automobile Business Entertainment Expense Log

Date 19 __	Place of Entertainment	Who Was Entertained/ Company, Title, or Occupation	Business Purpose or Benefit Expected or Received	Direct Entertainment Expenses					Total This Trip
				Auto Use	Food & Beverages	Parking & Tolls			
1/22	The Grill	J. Franklin, J. Evans Indep. sales reps	sub-rep agreement	14 70	55 82	1 00			71 52
Note: See page 66 for instructions on using this log and page 43 for information about using an auto for entertainment purposes.			Subtotals						

Automobile Business Entertainment Expense Log

Date 19 __	Place of Entertainment	Who Was Entertained/ Company, Title, or Occupation	Business Purpose or Benefit Expected or Received	Direct Entertainment Expenses						Total This Trip
				Auto Use	Food & Beverages	Parking & Tolls				
Note: See page 66 for instructions on using this log and page 43 for information about using an auto for entertainment purposes.			**Totals for Year**							

Casualty & Theft Loss Information

Description of Property & Loss Where Located	Date		1 Cost or Other Basis	2 Depr. Allowed or Allowable	3 Salvage Value if Totally Destroyed	4 Adjusted Basis 1−(2+3)	5 Reimb. Received or Expected	6 Gain, if Applic. (5) − (4)	Fair Market Value			Loss (Lesser of 4 or 9, and Less 5)
	Acquired	Loss or Discovery							7 Before Loss	8 After Loss	9 Decrease (7)−(8)	

Note: Transfer information to Form 4684 (Sec. A for personal losses, Sec. B for business losses). Limitations of $100 and 10% of AGI are reflected on Form 4684.

If asset was used for both business and pleasure, allocate loss based on percentage of business use at time of loss or more recent known percentage.

Self-Reimbursement Form for Expenses Paid in Cash

Description of Expense	From 1/1 to 1/15		From to	From to	From to	From to	From to	From to	From to	From to	From to	From to	From to	From to
Gasoline	$22	66												
Oil & Lube	2	25												
Wash & Wax	3	00												
Repairs & Maintenance	18	61												
Tires & Batteries	—													
Other Auto Supplies	4	67												
Taxi & Local Fares	—													
Parking Fees	6	50												
Tolls	8	00												
Telephone Calls	11	40												
Amount of Check	$77	09												
Date of Check	1/19													
Note: See page 67 for instructions. Check #	186													

Self-Reimbursement Form for Expenses Paid in Cash

Description of Expense	From to	From to	From to	From to	From to	From to	From to	From to	From to	From to	From to	From to	From to
Gasoline													
Oil & Lube													
Wash & Wax													
Repairs & Maintenance													
Tires & Batteries													
Other Auto Supplies													
Taxi & Local Fares													
Parking Fees													
Tolls													
Telephone Calls													
Amount of Check													
Date of Check													
Note: See page 67 for instructions. Check #													

Reimbursements Received from Others

Date 19 __	Received from	Reason for Payment	Amount Received		Date 19 __	Received from	Reason for Payment	Amount Received	
						Note: See page 46 for more information.	Total for Year		

128

Computation of Total Automobile Deduction Using Standard Mileage Rate

Computation of Business Use Percentage		Your Deduction		Example
Total Business/Investment Miles Driven from Summary on Page 87 . . . . (A)				18,306
Total Miles Driven from Summary on Page 87 . . . . (B)				22,162
Business Use Percentage (A) ÷ (B) . . . . (C)			%	82.6 %
Computation of Total Auto Deduction				
Mileage				
Multiply (B) or 15,000 Miles (Whichever Is Smaller) by 21¢		$		$ 3,150 00
Multiply Excess of (B) over 15,000 Miles by 11¢				363 66
For Autos Considered Fully Depreciated, Multiply (B) by 11¢				
Partially Deductible Expenses				
Interest on Auto Loan × (C)				941 64
Personal Property Taxes (Where Applicable) × (C)				
Other Expenses _____ × (C)				206 50
_____ × (C)				
_____ × (C)				
_____ × (C)				
Fully Deductible Expenses				
Business Parking Fees				410 00
Business Tolls				145 00
Other Expenses _____				
_____				
Note: See page 68 for instructions and page 17 for more information on this method.	**Total Auto Deduction for Year 19____**	$		$ 5,216 80

Computation of BUP & Total Automobile Deduction Using Actual Cost Method

Expenses per Annual Summary of Auto Expense Register		
Gasoline	$	
Oil		
Lubrication		
Wash & Wax		
Repairs & Maintenance		
Tires & Batteries		
Other Supplies		
Insurance		
Taxes		
Licenses		
Interest		
Garage Rent		
Auto Club Dues & Fees		
Miscellaneous Expenses		
Depreciation from Page 71		
Total Automobile Expenses Subject to Allocation (G)	$	

Computation of Business Use Percentages		
Computation for Meeting 50% Test		
Total Miles Driven for Qualified Trade or Business (A)		
Total Miles Driven for All Purposes During Year (B)		
Qualified Business Use Percentage (A) ÷ (B) (C)		%
Computation for Calculating Basis & Deductions		
Qualified Trade or Business Miles (A)		
Total Miles Driven for Investment/Production of Income (D)		
Total Business/Invest./Prod. of Income Miles (A) + (D) (E)		
BUP for Calculating Basis & Deductions (E) ÷ (B) (F)		%

Computation of Total Auto Deduction		
Total Allocated Business Expenses (G) × (F)	$	
Business Parking Fees & Tolls (Deductible in Full)	$	
Total Auto Deduction for Year 19 _____	$	

Note: See page 20 for more information on the actual cost method.

Tax Help

Choosing & Working with a Tax Advisor

Many taxpayers hire a tax advisor to prepare their return. Even if you do your own return, you may need the help of a professional tax advisor to solve a particular problem, to prepare for an IRS audit, or to plan for the future. You'll want to choose a qualified advisor you can trust and work with comfortably and confidently.

Who can be a tax advisor? There are more than 20,000 accounting firms in the U.S., and many thousands of people called tax preparers. Only a handful of states require tax preparers to take classes or be licensed.

It's best to retain someone who can legally represent you at all IRS levels. Generally, this person will be a CPA, an attorney, or an "enrolled agent." An enrolled agent must apply to the IRS, pass an examination, and be approved by the IRS to represent taxpayers. Unenrolled tax preparers may represent their clients *only* at the examination level.

Only CPAs, attorneys, and enrolled agents may perform the following on behalf of any taxpayer:

1. Execute claims for a refund.
2. Receive checks in payment of any refund of taxes, penalties, or interest.
3. Execute consents to extend the statutory period for assessment or collection of a tax.
4. Execute closing agreements with respect to a tax liability or specific matter.
5. Delegate authority or substitute another representative.

Fees paid for these services are deductible. Effective in 1987, taxpayers can only deduct them as a miscellaneous deduction, subject to a 2% floor.

Selecting your tax advisor. Many taxpayers don't take the selection process seriously enough. Be cautious and do your homework before you choose. Remember—if your tax preparer makes a mistake or files your return late, it's *you* who will have to pay any additional taxes, penalties, and interest.

Your goals are to find someone who will charge you a fair fee, not do anything that will cause an audit, and be genuinely interested in maximizing your tax savings. Ask friends or business associates whose tax situations might be similar to yours for recommendations, but don't rely on this alone. Do some investigating yourself, check references, and, above all, ask questions.

Before committing yourself, arrange a brief get-acquainted meeting and ask questions such as these:

- What are your areas of tax specialization?
- How do you keep up to date on tax matters?
- What continuing tax education have you undertaken?
- What is your previous tax experience?

Make sure you feel comfortable with the person but be patient—creating a good working relationship can take time.

If you have difficulty finding a competent professional, contact the American Institute of Certified Public Accountants in New York City or the National Society of Public Accountants in Alexandria, Virginia. They can supply you with names of members in good standing in your immediate area.

Some common pitfalls to avoid include retaining anyone who guarantees you a refund or who urges you to claim deductions to which you know you're not entitled, and hiring anyone who bases their fee on the amount of your refund.

Working with a professional. It's important not to just dump your tax records on your tax preparer's desk and have the preparer organize them for you. It will cost you money in increased fees. For best results, follow these guidelines:

- Present all your records in an orderly manner, categorized and summarized (or as requested by the tax preparer).
- Ask about hourly rates and other expenses of people working on your return, and find out how you might help minimize fees.
- Meet the staff people working on your return.
- Ask to receive copies of any correspondence related to you and ask for explanations for each claimed amount you don't understand.
- Before you sign your return, read each line carefully and compare the figures to your own wherever possible. And *never* sign an incomplete return.

133

- Make sure the tax preparer signs the return that is filed and that you receive a copy.
- If you're being audited, discuss with your tax advisor beforehand how much of each deduction under review may be allowed. Then you'll know when you can be flexible and when you need to stand your ground.
- Before you receive your tax advisor's final bill, ask that any portion of the bill that is not tax-deductible be detailed, to avoid any IRS disallowances.

Other rules and preparers' penalties. According to the IRS code, tax return preparers are subject to criminal penalties if they make an unauthorized disclosure of tax return information or use such information for any purpose other than to prepare a return. There are also penalties for understatement of taxpayer liability. And penalties are assessable for failing to meet the following requirements, unless the failure is due to reasonable cause and not willful neglect:

1. The return must be signed by the person primarily responsible for preparing the return and must also indicate the preparer's and/or firm's identifying number.

2. At the time the return is presented for signing, the taxpayer must be provided with a completed copy of the final return, though this copy need not be signed by the preparer.

3. For 3 years, preparers must keep available for IRS inspection a record of the name, taxpayer ID number, and principal place of work of each tax preparer who worked for them during the period.

4. Effective in 1985, preparers required to sign returns must advise taxpayers of the substantiation requirements of Section 274(d) of the code, related to travel and entertainment expenses, business gifts, and certain depreciation deductions. Preparers should receive assurances that such substantiation exists, but it need not be in writing.

These and other legal requirements have been established by Congress to protect the public against incompetent and dishonest tax preparers. Your awareness of these requirements can help you protect yourself. ∎

Most taxpayers' contact with the IRS is minimal—they file their return and pay their tax or receive a refund, whichever applies. But subsequently, some taxpayers learn that their return has been selected for an audit for any one of a number of reasons. The sections that follow will help you in this and any other dealings with the IRS.

Filing & Amending Your Return

Often, the procedures for filing a return and amending a previously filed return are not well known. Here is some information that may help you.

Filing your return. Always be sure to fill out your return completely, sign it, and file it on time. There are penalties both for late filing and nonpayment, so even if you can't pay then, be sure to send in your return on time.

If you can't make the filing deadline, you can get an automatic 4-month extension by filing Form 4868 and an additional 2-month extension if you have an acceptable reason. You'll be asked to estimate and pay the tax due when filing the extension. If you can't pay the full tax that's due, the IRS will accept an installment payment plan; you'll need to fill out all the necessary papers and agree to a monthly payment plan.

Filing penalties don't apply to a taxpayer entitled to a refund. Also, penalties for late payment can be waived if you have reasonable cause for not paying your tax when due.

Filing an amended return. Whenever you feel the tax you paid, whether resulting from an audit or some other reason, is excessive or incorrect, you have the right to file a claim for a refund. Check first, however, to be sure that no previous form you signed precludes you from filing such a claim. Individual taxpayers should use Form 1040X to file their claims. If you're amending a return for a prior year, you'll need to attach a copy.

You must file an amended return within 3 years of filing the original return or within 2 years

135

from the date you paid any tax, whichever is later. (If you filed earlier than the due date, it's considered as filed on the due date.)

If you have any complaints about the IRS, call their nearest office to find out where you should write. Two IRS publications which contain a lot of useful information are Publication 910: *Taxpayer's Guide to IRS Information, Assistance, and Publications* and Publication 586A: *The Collection Process (Income Tax Accounts)*.

The Audit & Appeals Process

The job the IRS performs year-round in issuing regulations and tax forms, collecting tax returns and payments, auditing the results, and sending out refunds is indeed awesome. Often, the job is done efficiently and rapidly. But some taxpayers have found just the reverse to be true. Repetitive audits, computer breakdowns, demands for taxes not owed, and misinformation are just some of the complaints taxpayers have made about the IRS.

What you need to learn from this is not to feel threatened if you're being audited by the IRS. As long as you're armed with tax knowledge, good

records, and the necessary documentation, you can feel perfectly confident when questioned. The IRS is much less likely to spend audit time on you than on someone with poor records or no records at all.

How returns are selected for audit. Since an average of only 25 out of every 1,000 tax returns are selected each year, most taxpayers never get audited. Don't think that just because you *are* selected you're suspected of being dishonest. Also don't think that because you received your refund you won't be audited. A look at the information below will help explain the selection process:

1. The majority of all selected returns (approximately 75%) come from a computer program called Discriminant Function System (DIF) which attaches a certain score to every line on your return. The computer compares your return with averages of other taxpayers in your tax bracket and attaches a line-by-line score. The higher your score above their predetermined minimum, the more likely you are to be selected.

2. The Taxpayer Compliance Measurement Program (TCMP) is a totally random-sample

selection process. The sample for the entire nation is small (about 50,000), but you might call it the unlucky lottery system. It's a time-consuming examination where you'll be expected to prove *every* item on your return.

3. In the matching documents method, computers match income information supplied to the IRS on forms (such as the W-2 and 1099) with information on taxpayers' returns.

4. Certain target groups, such as designated occupations and tax shelters, are selected from time to time for auditing.

5. Unusual fluctuations or changes in income or expenses could flag your return for audit. Travel and entertainment expenses have always been a popular audit subject.

6. Tips from informants, often ex-spouses or unhappy ex-employees, can trigger an audit.

7. Repetitive audits are legal as long as the previous one resulted in additional tax due. However, if the same items in a previous year resulted in no change in liability, you can probably get the audit suspended.

If your return shows some unusual or large amounts that you feel could target your return for auditing, attach proof for the amounts directly to your return, along with a narrative explanation. Always make sure all income is declared, so there will be no discrepancy between your return and information already supplied to the IRS. Generally, the IRS can audit your returns for the 3 previous years. If fraud is suspected or no return is filed, it can go back to any year.

How to prepare for an audit. The principal reasons the IRS disallows deductions are incomplete records and inadequate substantiation for claimed expenses. Provide the proof and all you'll need is a lot of patience to survive an audit. It also helps if you can communicate using *their* terms and if you understand tax law as much as possible.

You'll have to decide whether to handle the audit yourself or have a qualified professional represent you. If the issues are simple and the amounts involved are small, try it alone. If not, get help (see page 132 for information on how to select a tax advisor). You should, however, compare the potential tax savings with your advisor's estimated fees. When large amounts of tax are at stake, a professional may achieve a quicker resolution and a more favorable one for you as well.

Regardless of who deals with the IRS, here are some suggestions which will be of help:

1. If possible, insist that the entire matter be handled by correspondence and telephone. This allows you to stick to the issues, avoid personality conflicts, and resolve the audit more quickly.

2. If it must be in person, be familiar with your return, especially the items in question. IRS agents are under a lot of pressure to reach an agreement at the first meeting, so use this to your advantage by bringing everything you might possibly need to prove each item.

3. If the item in question is in a gray area, be aggressive, especially if your records are complete. Argue that you're supplying exactly what the law requires.

4. With prior approval, you can tape-record all meetings, and so can the IRS.

5. And now for the don'ts. Don't try to be buddies with the agent or, conversely, get angry. Don't volunteer any information—just answer the questions. Don't sign anything until you've had a lot of time to review it (with professional help), because once you sign a consent form, there's no appeal.

If you and the agent agree, it's over. If you don't, ask to see the agent's supervisor, who may be easier to deal with in reaching a final agreement.

The appeals process. The IRS has established an elaborate system of appeals which offers you a wide variety of options. If you didn't reach an agreement with the agent's supervisor, your next stop, and the only one still within the IRS, is the Appeals Office in your region. It's very informal—you can represent yourself if you like—and most audits are resolved at this level. This is because the appeals officer can bargain with you, so be aware that negotiation will be a constant activity from this point forward. There can be good-faith settlement offers and counteroffers on both sides.

The higher the authority, the more likely the compromise—the IRS wants to settle as much as you. For information about this and other related subjects, ask your local IRS office for Publication 556: *Examination of Returns, Appeal Rights, and Claims for Refund.*

Keep in mind that at any stage of the appeal procedure you can do any of the following:

1. Agree and arrange to pay the tax.
2. Ask the IRS to send you a notice of deficiency in order for you to file a petition with the Tax Court.
3. Pay the tax and immediately file a claim for a refund.

The court system. More and more taxpayers are settling disputes with the IRS through litigation. The number of new cases has more than doubled in the past 5 years, resulting in a large backlog.

The Tax Court will only hear your case if the disputed tax has not been assessed or paid. If it has been paid and you've filed for a refund, you must file suit either in the U.S. District Court or the U.S. Court of Claims. You may represent yourself or have an attorney or someone else admitted to practice before that court represent you.

Tax$aver Tip. If the dispute involves $10,000 or less (including taxes and penalties) for any one tax year, you can have it handled as a "small tax case." The advantages are that you can represent yourself, a final binding decision can be rendered with a minimum of expense and delay, trial judges have much latitude as to the rules of evidence, and the proceedings are simple and informal.

No formal written opinion is issued, and the decision can't be used as a precedent by other taxpayers. But you give up your right to appeal if the decision goes against you. For a petition form and other information, write to the Clerk of the Court, U.S. Tax Court, 400 Second Street, NW, Washington, D.C. 20217. ∎

139

Glossary of IRS Terms

Accelerated cost recovery system (ACRS): A system of depreciating most business assets that's required for all assets placed in service after 1980; requires use of defined time periods and percentages to claim the deduction instead of estimating the asset's useful life.

Accelerated depreciation: Any method of deducting the cost of an asset at a faster rate than straight-line (pro rata) depreciation.

Actual cost method (ACM): A method for claiming automobile operating costs that requires the taxpayer to keep detailed records of each item of expense, including depreciation. The total (not including parking fees and tolls) is multiplied by the percentage of business use applicable to the car.

Adjusted basis: The actual cost of an asset (basis) plus any additions, such as major improvements made, and less any reductions, such as depreciation claimed.

Associated with test: Expenses for entertainment are deductible if considered associated with the active conduct of a trade or business; clear business purpose in making the expenditure must be established, in addition to its being ordinary and necessary.

Away from home: Any period of time longer than an ordinary work day which includes time for sleep and rest.

Business associate: Any person with whom a taxpayer could reasonably expect to engage or deal in the active conduct of a trade or business, such as a customer, client, supplier, employee, agent, partner, or professional advisor, whether established or prospective.

Business entertainment: Covers any trade- or business-connected activity generally considered to constitute entertainment; also covers recreation and amusement activities.

Business relationship test: There must be a proximate relationship to business or to business benefits to meet this test.

Business use percentage (BUP): A percentage determined by dividing business use (either in miles or time) by total miles or time available for all uses.

Capital expenditure: A major addition or improvement to property, such as an air conditioner for a car, that's permanent in nature, increases the value or extends the life of the property, and cannot be deducted in the year incurred (it must be depreciated).

Convenience of employer test: This test is satisfied if an employer requires an employee to use something, such as a car, as a condition of employment in order to properly perform the employee's duties.

Depreciation: The systematic allocation of the cost of an asset over some period of time by various methods.

Directly related test: Entertainment is considered directly related to business when all the following requirements are satisfied:

1. At the time the taxpayer had more than a *general expectation* of deriving income or other business benefit at some future date (not merely goodwill). Income or benefit does not have to result from each expenditure.
2. During the entertainment period, the taxpayer was *actively engaged* in a business meeting, discussion, or transaction with the person(s) being entertained.
3. The principal purpose of the entertainment was business and not only incidental to it.
4. The money spent was allocable to the person(s) with whom the taxpayer engaged in the active conduct of trade or business during the entertainment.

Other ways of satisfying this test are not relevant to auto use.

Employee: Someone subject to the will and control of an employer as to what and when work is done.

Fair market value: An amount which would influence a willing seller to sell and a willing buyer to buy, each with no pressure to do so.

Listed property: Depreciable business property used as a means of transportation; any property of

141

a type generally used for purposes of entertainment, recreation, or amusement; and any other property specified by the regulations and purchased or leased and placed in service after June 18, 1984.

Ordinary and necessary: An expenditure is *ordinary* if it is a common and accepted practice in a particular trade or business; to be *necessary*, it should be appropriate and helpful in the performance, promotion, or furtherance of a trade or business. *Necessary* does not mean absolutely essential, but it also can't be unreasonable.

Outside sales: The business of selling and soliciting, away from the employer's place of business, the products or services of the employer.

Per diem allowance: A fixed amount of money allowed by an employer for daily away-from-home expenses, such as meals, lodging, laundry, cleaning, and tips.

Placed in service: The date property, such as a car, is in a condition or state of readiness and is available for a specifically assigned use.

Recapture rule: When tax benefits claimed under certain rules for depreciation and investment tax credit have to be paid back because of something that occurs in a later year, such as an early disposition of the asset or because the BUP 50% test is no longer being met.

Repairs: Expenditures to keep property in good condition but which do not increase the value or prolong its useful life. If business related, the expenditures are deductible in the year paid.

Standard mileage rate method (SMR): An optional method for claiming automobile operating costs whereby the total miles driven for business or investment use are multiplied by an IRS-approved rate, currently 21¢ per mile for the first 15,000 miles. A rate of 11¢ per mile applies for additional mileage and for fully depreciated cars.

Straight-line depreciation: A method of deducting the cost of an asset equally each year over its estimated useful life.

Substantial business discussion: When business is combined with entertainment, it must be established that a business meeting, negotiation, discussion, or transaction was substantial compared to the entertainment. The business activity should be for deriving income or other specific business benefits. It is not necessary that more time be devoted to business than to entertainment to meet these requirements. All facts and circumstances will be considered.

Tax home: Main place of business, regardless of where the family home is located; entire city or area where business is located.

Tax preparer: Any person who prepares income tax returns for compensation or who employs others to do so. Preparing a return means obtaining information, determining which tax rules apply and how they should be applied, computing the tax, and completing the forms.

Trade or business: Any activity carried on for livelihood or for profit and where there is some type of economic activity involved. It is characterized by the regularity of such activities and transactions and by the production of income.

Transportation expenses: The cost to get from one point to another, as differentiated from "travel expenses," which include meals and lodging while away from home.

Useful life: The expected, reasonable number of years that an asset is used in a trade or business or for the production of income. ■

Index